I0233550

STORIES

of the Friends of Allah ﷻ

By Maulana Abun-Nūr Muhammad Bashīr ﷺ

HEDAAYA Publications

Stories of the Friends of Allah ﷻ

Second Edition (August 2012) by **Hedaaya Publications** – Greytown, South Africa. E-mail **hedaaya.publications@gmail.com** for information on other publications (or see back of book).

All Rights Reserved. No part of this book may be reproduced or transmitted by any means, electronic or mechanical, without written permission from the publisher.

ISBN 978-0-620-54261-6

الا ان اولياء الله لا خوف عليهم ولا هم يحزنون

*"Behold! Indeed the **Friends of Allah** ﷻ have no fear*
nor do they grieve."
– Surah Yunus (10), Verse 62

اتقوا فراسة المؤمن فانه ينظر بنور الله

"Beware the perception of a true believer, for indeed
he sees with the noor of Allah ﷻ."
– The Holy Prophet ﷺ

WHO ARE THE FRIENDS OF ALLAH ﷻ?

The Friends of Allah ﷻ are certain individuals who have gained a special closeness to Allah ﷻ after immersing themselves in complete obedience to Him. This is not a position that is self-acquired, but one that is *bestowed* upon them, and it can happen in an instant or after proving oneself for decades on end. After the Prophets, they are the greatest in the kingdom of Allah ﷻ.

Throughout history, these 'Saints' have helped assist the Muslim Ummah, physically and spiritually, to rid itself of whichever evils plagued it in their respective eras, and they were (and are) usually at the forefront of Islamic change.

Hadrat Sulaiman عليه السلام once wanted the throne of the Queen of Sheba brought to him, which was huge and said to be over 1,500 miles away. After gathering his entire kingdom together, he asked the leaders of each division,

يايها الملوا ايكم ياتيني بعرشها قبل ان يأتوني مسلمين

"O Chiefs! Which of you can bring the throne to me before
they come to me in submission?"
– Surah Naml (27), Verse 38

قال عفريت من الجن أنا آتيك به قبل أن تقوم من مقامك

And evil Jinn replied, "[O Sulaiman!] I will bring it to you
before you rise from your council."
– Surah Naml (27), Verse 39

One man, however (whom the Quran describes as a scholar, not a Prophet), said to him,

أنا آتيك به قبل أن يرتد إليك طرفك

*"[O Sulaiman!] I will bring it to you before the **blinking of an eye**."*
– Surah Naml (27), Verse 40

And indeed, in just the twinkling of an eye, Hadrat Asif Barkhia رضي الله عنه arrived with the throne of Bilkees and placed it before Hadrat Sulaiman عليه السلام (a minute example of the power granted by Allah ﷻ to these majestic individuals).

Furthermore, the Holy Quran not only mentions stories of the Saints themselves, but gives us a glimpse of how highly they are regarded in the sight of their Lord.

Allah ﷻ states,

إن الصفا والمروة من شعائر الله

"Certainly, Safaa and Marwa are amongst the signs of Allah ﷻ."
– Surah Baqarah (2), Verse 158

What makes Safaa and Marwaa so important that Allah ﷻ has taken them as two of His signs? Indeed, it was the running of Sayyidah Hājirah رضي الله عنها between these two places that came to be the beloved practice of Allah ﷻ by one of his *Friends* (not Prophets), a practice so liked by Him that no Muslim until today will have his or her Hajj accepted unless they imitate this action of hers.

If Safaa and Marwaa (originally two unassuming hills) could both become the signs of Allah ﷻ simply by having a *connection* to a Saint, what can possibly be said now of the Saints themselves?!

A popular question asked nowadays is, "Without direct indication from the Quran & Hadith, how do we know that the people we take as contemporary Friends of Allah ﷻ are truly that?"

One answer to this is that we testify to things everyday without direct instruction from the Quran & Hadith, such as whether someone is a Muslim or not, whether a new activity is permissible or impermissible, whether a certain dish is Halaal or Haraam, etc. We're constantly taking what we know to be Islam and applying it to things all around us, and the Muslim Ummah will never agree on something that's incorrect,

وكذلك جعلناكم أمة وسطا لتكونوا شهداء على الناس

"We have made you the just nation so that you may give witness on people."
– Surah Baqarah (2), Verse 143

4

ما راه المؤمنون حسنا فهو عند الله حسن

"Whatever is deemed good by Muslims is good in the sight of Allah ﷻ."
– Hadith Sharif

With this in mind, the following is a collection of incidents regarding some of the most renowned Saints in the history of Islam (focusing mainly on those in the Arabian Peninsula). It is a partial translation of a compilation by Hadrat Abun-Nūr Muhammad Bashīr ؒ, and we request Allah ﷻ to have mercy on him and to use this work to better instill the knowledge, recognition and respect of His Friends within the English speaking Muslim community. *Ameen!*

بسم الله الرحمن الرحيم
نحمده و نصلي على رسوله الكريم

لقد كان في قصصهم عبرة لأولي الألباب

"There is, in their stories, instruction for men endued with understanding."
– Surah Yusuf (12), Verse 111

1 – HADRAT UWAIS QARNI ﷺ

As the demise of the Holy Prophet ﷺ neared, his Companions asked him, "O Rasoolullah ﷺ, who should we give your blessed garment to?"
He replied, "Uwais Qarni ﷺ."

And so, after Rasoolullah's ﷺ demise, Hadrat Umar ﷺ and Hadrat Ali ﷺ travelled to Yemen and asked the people there if anyone lived in the area of Qarn. They replied, "Yes."
When they asked about a person by the name of Uwais Qarni ﷺ, the people said that although they didn't know him personally, there *was* someone by that name who lived in the jungle away from the populated area and was considered a madman. Hadrat Umar ﷺ replied, "Take us to him."

When the two Companions reached the place, they found Hadrat Uwais Qarni ﷺ busy in Salaah and sat waiting for him to finish.
When he did, they greeted him and he returned their Salaam.
Hadrat Umar ﷺ then asked him what his name was. He replied, "My name is Uwais ﷺ."
He also asked him to put out his right hand, and when Hadrat Uwais Qarni ﷺ did so, they saw on it the sign that the Holy Prophet ﷺ had spoken to them about.
Hadrat Umar ﷺ then kissed his hand and said, "We bring good news that the Prophet ﷺ himself sends his Salaam to you, wishes that you have his blessed garment, and requests that you make dua for his Ummah."
Hearing this, Hadrat Uwais Qarni ﷺ went into a state of ecstasy, walked away from the two Companions and went into sajda (in another part of the house), saying, "O Creator of Love and Lover of Your Beloved (i.e. Allah ﷻ)! Your Beloved ﷺ has sent his blessed garment to this loving beggar. With Your permission, I ask that You allow him to wear it."
A voice was then heard saying, "Yes, wear it."

Hadrat Uwais Qarni ﷺ continued, "O Allah ﷻ, I will not wear it until you forgive the *entire* Ummah of Your Beloved ﷺ!"

When the voice said that a few thousand were forgiven, the Saint replied, "O Allah ﷻ, forgive as many as there are threads in this garment."

When it was said that *twice* as many were forgiven, he maintained, "O Allah ﷻ, I will not wear it until all are forgiven!"

Allah ﷻ then said, "I have forgiven many thousands."

Hadrat Uwais ﷺ persisted, "I wish for all!"

During this extraordinary conversation, Hadrat Umar ﷺ and Hadrat Ali ﷺ came to see what was happening and were then asked by Hadrat Uwais Qarni ﷺ, "Why did you two come?! I will never wear this until the *entire Ummah* is forgiven!"

After some time, he eventually put on the garment and said, "With my intercession and the blessings of this garment, for every hair amongst the sheep of the Rabee'a and Midhr tribes, someone in the Ummah will be forgiven."

Unable to contain his joy, he then began to cry uncontrollably.

Seeing the magnificence and manner of this astonishing individual, Hadrat Umar ﷺ and Hadrat Ali ﷺ began to cry too. They then asked him, "With all your love and enthusiasm for the Prophet ﷺ, what stopped you from ever meeting him?"

Hadrat Uwais ﷺ replied, "You both say you've seen Rasoolullah ﷺ. Tell me, do his eyebrows join in the middle or are they separate from one another?"

When the two Companions were seen unable to give any answer to this, Hadrat Uwais ﷺ began to perfectly describe the blessed eyebrows of the Holy Prophet ﷺ to them. He then ended his conversation by saying, "Even though I'm not physically present in his service, I'm still not detached from the reflection of the Beloved ﷺ." – *Tazkiratul-Auliya, Pg. 24*

Lesson Hadrat Uwais Qarni ﷺ possesses a truly elevated status, that even though he never saw the Holy Prophet ﷺ with his physical eyes, his inner-self was still blessed with the sight of his beauty and splendor. We come to know from this that for those who have great love for the Prophet ﷺ, he is forever in front of their inner, spiritual eyes.

Also, we see that from just a piece of clothing touching the blessed body of Rasoolullah ﷺ, *and* from the duas of the pious, we as Muslims gain forgiveness from our sins.

Supplementary Those fortunate to have seen the Prophet ﷺ with their physical eyes are known as the *Sahaabah*, and those who didn't see him but saw the Sahaaba are known as the *Taabi'een*. So, Hadrat Uwais Qarni ﷺ is amongst the Taabi'een, and was even described by the Prophet ﷺ as خير التابعين (the best of them). – *Miskhaat, Pg. 574*

Even though he lived in the time of Rasoolullah ﷺ, he never physically saw him because his mother was old and weak (and so he was unable to leave her). – *Haashiatu-Mishkaat, Pg. 574*

Nevertheless, for his consolation, Rasoolullah ﷺ told his Companions (in demonstrating Hadrat Uwais Qarni's ﷺ greatness and glory), " من لقيه منكم فليستغفر لكم Whoever from amongst you meets him should ask him to make dua for forgiveness for you."

يوم ندعو كل أناس بإمامهم

"One day We will call together all humans with their respective Imams."
– Surah Isra (17), Verse 71

2 – IMAM ABU HANIFA ﷺ & THE ATHEIST

Imam Abu Hanifa ﷺ and an atheist (one who denies the existence of Allah ﷻ) were to once meet somewhere and debate on this very issue. On the stipulated day, everyone gathered to witness the event (including the atheist), but the great Imam was nowhere to be seen.

After some time, he finally arrived and was asked by his opponent, "What took you so long?"

Imam Abu Hanifa ﷺ replied, "If I told you that on the way here, I saw something amazing and stood in awe of it – that there was a tree on a riverbank which got cut, fell to the ground, assembled itself into planks, from planks became a ship, and as a ship sailed on the river, taking passengers and dropping them off after accepting their fares, all without the help of anyone – would you believe me?"

The atheist laughed and replied, "Such a leader yet you speak such crazy things, saying that all of this could've happened without someone to carry these procedures out."

Imam Abu Hanifa ﷺ then said, "If that's impossible, isn't it even stranger to think that the entire universe has been assembled without the help of anyone? That this earth, this sky, this sun, these stars, these gardens, these flowers & fruits, these mountains, and all humans and animals just came into being without the work of a creator? If, according to you, only a tree turning into a ship without a coordinator is a lie, wouldn't saying *'the entire universe* came into being without a coordinator' be an even bigger one?"

Astonished upon hearing this, the atheist then repented for his previous beliefs and immediately embraced the deen of Islam. – *Tafseer Kabeer, Vol. 1, Pg. 221*

3 – THE LEADER OF THE MUSLIMS, IMAM ABU HANIFA ﷺ

Imam Abu Hanifa ﷺ once traveled to Madina to present himself in front of the Holy Prophet ﷺ. When he reached the sacred Rauda, he said, " السلام عليك يا سيد المرسلين Peace be upon you, O Leader of the Prophets."

11

A voice was then heard from the Rauda saying, "وعليك السلام يا امام للمسلمين And peace be upon you, O Leader of the Muslims!" – *Tazkiratul-Auliya, Pg. 246*

Lesson We come to know that the Holy Prophet 📿 is alive, hears the greeting of Muslims, and answers them too.

We also see that Imam Abu Hanifa 📿 is the Leader of the Muslims – a title not self-bestowed, but one given to him by the Beloved Prophet of Allah 📿 himself. If anyone now insults the integrity of the great Imam, will Allah 📿 and His Beloved 📿 not be angry with him?

4 – A RESPECTED OLD MAN

Hadrat Shaikh Bu Ali ibn Uthman Jalaali 📿 narrates, "I once presented myself at the *qabr* of Hadrat Bilal 📿 in Syria and fell asleep there. In a dream, I was in Makkah and saw the Holy Prophet 📿 enter the Bani Shaiba door while assisting an elderly man with love and support. I ran towards the Prophet 📿, kissed his feet and thought, "Who's this man he's walking with?"

The Prophet 📿 naturally knew what I was thinking and replied, "This is the Imam of the Muslims, Abu Hanifa 📿." – *Tazkiratul-Auliya, Pg. 252*

Lesson We come to know that the *muzhab* of Imam Abu Hanifa 📿 is endorsed and supported by the Holy Prophet 📿 himself.

5 – THE RESPONSIBILITY OF A LEADER

Once, while Imam Abu Hanifa 📿 was going somewhere, he saw a young girl walking in mud and said to her, "Girl, walk carefully, or your foot will get stuck and you'll fall."

She replied, "O Imam 📿, I'm walking alone. What does it matter if I fall? I'll just get up and carry on. You, on the other hand, are the Leader of the Muslims, and you shouldn't forget that. If you fall, the *entire* Muslim Ummah who is behind you will fall too, and recovering from that will be very difficult."

Hearing this, Imam Abu Hanifa 📿 began to cry. – *Tazkiratul-Auliya, Pg. 250*

Lesson Young or old, male or female, every Muslim accepts that Imam Abu Hanifa 📿 is our leader due to the great work he carried out in clarifying the rules of the Quran & Hadith for us (amongst many other contributions).

6 – THE IMAM WHO STAYS AWAKE THE ENTIRE NIGHT

Imam Abu Hanifa ؓ used to read 300 rakaats optional Salaah every night until he was once walking somewhere and heard someone say to his friend, "That's the Imam that reads 500 rakaats every night."

Not wanting people's view of him to be incorrect, he then decided to increase his Salaah to 500 rakaats, and continued reading this many until he was told by his students, "People say that you read Salaah *the entire night* and don't sleep."

The great Imam replied, "From now on, I'll do just that, because Allah ﷻ states that those who like being praised for things falsely attributed to them will not be saved from punishment. If I stay awake in worship, I won't fall under this verse."

So, from that day onwards, Imam Abu Hanifa ؓ read his Fajr Salaah with his wudhu for Esha Salaah every day for forty years! His place of demise was also where he'd completed *seven thousand* Quran Sharifs. – *Tazkiratul-Auliya, Pg. 249, Jawaahirul-Bayaan fi Tarjamatil-Khairaatil-Hisaan, Pg. 63*

Lesson Our Beloved Imam ؓ was not only the leader in Islamic Jurisprudence, but was also an unequaled example of how one should lead his or her life in this world.

7 – DIRT THE SIZE OF A FINGERNAIL

Imam Abu Hanifa ؓ was once walking in the bazaar when a small amount of dirt (the size of a fingernail) fell onto his clothes. He immediately proceeded to the edge of the Tigris River and began to wash it off. People saw this and said, "Imam ؓ! You're the one who told us that that much dirt on one's clothes is permissible, but now you're the one who's washing it off!"

He replied, "True, but that was *fatwa* (my verdict), and this is *taqwa* (piety)." – *Tazkiratul-Auliya, Pg. 151*

8 – CHIEF JUDGE

The Khalifa of his time, Mansoor, once summoned Imam Abu Hanifa ﷺ to his court and said, "I want you to accept the position of being my chief judge."

The Imam replied, "I'm incapable of such a position."

The Khalifa exclaimed, "Liar! If not you, who else can do it?!"

The great Imam answered, "If I'm truly a liar as you say, then the decision has been made. I cannot be your chief judge because liars are not fit to be judges."

He then turned around and walked away. – *Tazkiratul-Auliya, Pg. 248*

Lesson The Friends of Allah ﷺ are unimpressed by high worldly positions and ranks. How then can those who commit their entire lives to attaining such distinctions insult the integrity of these great personalities?

9 – UTMOST PIETY

Imam Abu Hanifa ﷺ once went somewhere to perform a Janaazah Salaah. The day was blistering hot and there was no shade anywhere except beside a house nearby. Seeing the great Imam standing under direct sunlight, some people asked him, "Imam ﷺ, why don't you stand in the shade?"

He replied, "No. The person who owns that house has taken a loan from me, and I fear that if I benefit by standing in his shade, I'll be included amongst those who dealt in interest, because the Holy Prophet ﷺ said, 'Whatever is gained from a loan is interest.'"

For this reason, the great Imam remained where he was. – *Tazkiratul-Auliya, Pg. 248*

Lesson We come to know here of the immense piety of Imam Abu Hanifa ﷺ and recognize that he always had the narrations of the Holy Prophet ﷺ guiding him in his decisions.

10 – THE EFFECT OF THE QURAN

The virtuous Hadrat Yazeed ibn Laith narrates, "Imam Abu Hanifa ﷺ and I were once reading Esha Salaah behind someone who read اذا زلزلت الارض (Surah 99, Zilzāl) in one of the rakaats. After the Salaah, I saw Imam Abu

Hanifa ﷺ sitting down breathing heavily with a concerned look on his face, and since I didn't wish to disturb him, I left a lamp burning close-by and then exited the musjid.

At the time of Fajr, I returned to the musjid and saw him *still there* clutching his beard and saying, "O You Who grants good for an atom's worth of good and You Who grants bad for an atom's worth of bad! (Referring to the last few verses of Surah Zilzāl) Save Nu'maan (i.e. Imam Abu Hanifa ﷺ) from the fire through Your Bounty. Keep him far away from it and place him in Your mercy!"

When I walked inside, the great Imam looked at me and asked, "Do you want the lamp?"

I answered, "I've already given the Azaan."

He then said, "Don't tell anyone what you just saw." – *Jawaahirul-Bayaan fi Tarjamatil-Khairaatil-Hisaan, Pg. 68*

11 – FEAR OF THE DAY OF JUDGMENT

Imam Abu Hanifa ﷺ once unknowingly stepped on a boy's foot and was told by him, "Shaikh! Don't you fear reimbursement on the Day of Qiyaamat?"

Hearing this, the great Imam fell to the floor unconscious.

When he awoke, he said, "I think those words were inspired to him." – *Jawaahirul-Bayaan, Pg. 69*

Lesson All of these examples show that Imam Abu Hanifa ﷺ lived in extreme fear of Allah ﷻ during his entire life. Can someone now say that he was not responsible and cautious in his verdicts?

12 – AN 'INSIGNIFICANT' NEIGHBOUR

There was a detested man in the eyes of the public who used to live next to Imam Abu Hanifa ﷺ. Every day he'd go to the market, buy some food and drinks and get drunk with his friends singing, "People have forsaken me, and what a personality they've lost! Someone who's useful in fights and in removing obstructions!"

Even though the Imam slept very little at night, he never complained about this.

One night, the chief of police arrived at the man's door and arrested him. When Imam Abu Hanifa ﷺ came to know of this from his students, he proceeded to the authorities of Kufa to speak about the matter and was greeted with great respect by its governor.

After seating the Imam, the governor said to him, "If you told me you wanted to see me, I would've come to you."

He replied, "A neighbour of mine was arrested last night. I wish for him to be set free."

As per his request, the governor allowed the man to be released, and as the man emerged from his jail cell, Imam Abu Hanifa ﷺ met with him and asked, "Have we forsaken you?"

He replied, "No. You have truly fulfilled the rights of a neighbour."

After witnessing the kindness and character of this Friend of Allah ﷻ, the man then repented for the life that he'd lived and began to attend the lessons and discourses given by the great Imam (until he himself became distinguished in the field of Islamic Jurisprudence). – *Hayawaatul-Haywaan, Vol. 1, Pg. 18*

Lesson Even in the worst of times, one should be caring towards one's neighbours (due to the amount of emphasis Islam has placed on them).

13 – KINDNESS

Hadrat Shafeeq ﷺ narrates, "Imam Abu Hanifa ﷺ and I were once walking somewhere when someone who was coming towards us saw the Imam, went quiet and quickly chose another path. Imam Abu Hanifa ﷺ called out to him and asked, "Why did you change pathways?"

The man replied, "Hadrat, I took a loan of 10,000 dinars from you and haven't paid it yet even though the prescribed time is over. I'm struggling for money at the moment and I can't bear to look at you out of shame."

Imam Abu Hanifa ﷺ replied, "Subhanallah! You're like this because of me?! Go. You don't have to pay me the money anymore, and I've made myself witness over my *nafs*. Don't hide from me from now onwards and forgive me if you're ever frightened for my sake again." – *Jawaahirul-Bayaan, Pg. 74*

Lesson The Friends of Allah ﷺ have no care for the world and always show kindness to the creation of Allah ﷻ. These are the qualities we should sincerely strive to adopt within ourselves in every moment of our lives.

A group of boys were once playing with a ball near a gathering of scholars (amongst whom was Imam Abu Hanifa ﷺ). The ball was unintentionally kicked near them and none of the boys had the courage to retrieve it except one (who cared not for the respect of Islamic Scholars).

Seeing him come and take the ball away, Imam Abu Hanifa ﷺ said to those around him, "This boy is not from permissible intercourse."

When the people made inquiries about this, they found it to be true and asked the great Imam how he knew.

He replied, "If he was from permissible intercourse, his modesty would've stopped him from doing what he did." – *Tazkiratul-Auliya*

Lesson Respecting the learned and showing humility in front of them is a sign of good manners and virtue.

15 – A SILENCING REPLY

Imam Abu Hanifa ﷺ was once asked by one of his detractors, "What would you say about a person who doesn't anticipate Jannah, doesn't fear Jahannam or Allah ﷻ, eats corpses, reads Salaah without ruku or sajda, testifies without seeing things, doesn't like the truth, befriends mischief, runs away from mercy, and accepts the sayings of Christians and Jews?"

The Imam first turned to his students and asked them, "What would you all say about such a person?"

They replied, "He'd be a terrible individual. These are the qualities of a kaafir."

The Imam then smiled and said, "No. Such a person is a Friend of Allah ﷻ and a complete believer."

He then turned to the man and asked him, "If I answer your question, will you stop slandering me?"

The man replied, "Yes, I promise."

Imam Abu Hanifa ﷺ then said, "Such a person doesn't anticipate Jannah because he anticipates meeting the *Creator* of Jannah. Likewise, he doesn't fear Jahannam, but fears the Creator of Jahannam. He doesn't fear Allah ﷻ in the sense that he knows he will not be treated unjustly by Him. The corpses he eats are those of fish, and the Salaah he reads without ruku and sajda is Janaazah Salaah. He gives testimony without seeing things by testifying to the existence of Allah ﷻ even though he has never seen Him. He doesn't like death even though it's the truth (since he wishes to live long and continue to obey his Lord). Money and children are both forms of mischief yet he befriends them. The mercy that he runs away from is *rain*, and the sayings of the Christians and Jews that he accepts is when they both said to each other, "You have naught to stand upon." (Referring to Surah Baqarah (2), Verse 113).

Hearing this magnificent and silencing reply, the man then stood up, kissed the head of the great Imam and said, "I swear that you are on the truth." – *Jawaahirul-Bayaan fi Tarjamatil-Khairaatil-Hisaan, Pg. 84*

Lesson Imam Abu Hanifa ﷺ was granted such great depth in understanding Islam that even his enemies acknowledged it.

16 – A CONVERSATION BETWEEN IMAM ABU HANIFA ﷺ & IMAM MALIK ﷺ

Imam Abu Hanifa ﷺ once left Iraq to sit amongst students being taught by Imam Malik ﷺ (unbeknownst to Imam Malik ﷺ who he was). When the students were asked a question concerning Islamic Law, Imam Abu Hanifa ﷺ answered it so calmly that it caught the attention of Imam Malik ﷺ, who asked his class, "Where's this person from?"
Imam Abu Hanifa ﷺ replied, "I came from Iraq."

"From the people of enmity and hypocrisy?"

"May I recite something?"

"Yes."

"Some of the desert Arabs around you are hypocrites, as well as amongst the people of Iraq." (In other words, Imam Abu Hanifa ﷺ read the 101st verse of Surah Tauba (9) but said 'people of Iraq' instead of 'people of the city', doing this to establish a proof against Imam Malik ﷺ.)

Imam Malik ﷺ replied, "That's not the verse!"

"Then how is the verse read?"

"It's 'Some of the desert Arabs around you are hypocrites, as well as amongst the people of *the city*.'"

Imam Abu Hanifa ﷺ then said, "Then I'm thankful to Allah ﷻ that he emplaced the same order over you as He did over me."

He then stood up and left the gathering.

When Imam Malik ﷺ came to know who this personality was, he immediately called the Imam back and began to show him great respect. – *Nuzhatul-Majaalis, Vol. 1, Pg. 137*

Lesson Imam Abu Hanifa ﷺ had a gift (given to him by Allah ﷻ) of giving spontaneous replies to people.

We also see that, even though the other Imams differed with him in many laws, they still recognized his great service rendered to the Ummah and showed the utmost of respect to him.

17 – CHANGING OF THE BRIDE*

A man once married his two sons to another man's two daughters and invited the public to a *waleemah* on the day after the wedding. During the feast, the father of the brides had an extremely uncomfortable look on his face and took the Islamic Scholars (which included Imam Abu Hanifa ﷺ) outside, saying to them, "A big mistake has been made. Last night, my two daughters slept with the wrong husbands and only came to know of this in the morning. What should we do?"

Hadrat Sufyaan ﷺ replied, "There's no problem here. What happened is classified as *wati-bish'uba*. The two brothers will simply have to give the dowry, and the sisters can then go back to their original husbands."

Hearing this, Imam Abu Hanifa ﷺ remained silent. Nevertheless, the father turned to him anyway and asked him, "Is there anything else that can be done?"

Hadrat Sufyaan ﷺ replied, "What else *is there* to do?"

Imam Abu Hanifa ﷺ then said, "Bring both the husbands to me."

When the brothers were then presented before him, Imam Abu Hanifa ﷺ asked them, "Do you like the women you spent the night with?"

They answered, "Yes."

The great Imam then said, "Then divorce your original wives and marry who you were with instead."

So, the two husbands did as they were advised, and since nothing had taken place between them and their original wives, there was no need for *iddat*, and the new nikaahs were performed immediately thereafter. – *Jawaahirul-Bayaan, Pg. 26*

Lesson Not only could Imam Abu Hanifa ؆ explain intricate laws of Shariah, he was even able to bring out the *best* of outcomes in it. It was this very outstanding intellect of his that helped simplify the hundreds of queries regarding Islamic Law and made it easier for the Ummah to understand it until today.

18 – SKYLIGHT

A man once wrote an application to the judge Qaazi Ibn Abil-Ulaa saying that he wished to insert a window into a wall of his but was being stopped from doing so by one of his neighbours. When the neighbour was summoned to give his reasoning for this, he presented such a strong argument in his case that the judge eventually ruled in his favour.

Imam Abu Hanifa ؆ soon heard about this and said to the man, "Now seek a permit to bring that wall down."

The man did as he was told, and since the owner of any wall has the right to bring his own property down, he was granted permission to do so and later announced this to everyone upon his return.

When his neighbour came to know of this new plan, he immediately ran to the judge and said, "That man now plans to bring the entire wall down! Give him permission to insert his window instead, because this will be easier for me."

So, the ruling was passed by the judge – as the neighbour wished! – *Jawaahirul-Bayaan, Pg. 88*

Lesson The great wisdom of Imam Abu Hanifa ؆ allowed him to solve the problems of the public without transgressing the borders of Islamic Law.

19 – A SOLVER OF ONE'S PROBLEMS

A neighbour of Imam Abu Hanifa ؆ once came to him and said, "I want to marry a girl but her family's asking for more dowry than I can provide. What can I do?"

In response, Imam Abu Hanifa ؆ read Istikhaara Salaah and later informed the man that he may marry said woman.

After the nikaah, the man was told by his in-laws that he wouldn't be given the bride until the dowry was paid. So, not knowing what to do, he went once again to Imam Abu Hanifa ﷺ and sought his assistance in the matter.

The great Imam replied, "Take loans from people and pay them off."

The Imam even gave some of his own wealth to the man and said to him the following day, "Now let your in-laws know that you're going with your wife far away from here."

The man did as he was instructed, and when his in-laws heard of his plans to move away, they approached the Imam complaining about this and sought a verdict against him.

The Imam replied, "He's the husband and can do as he pleases."

"But we can't bear our daughter to be so far from us!"

"Then why don't you return what you took from him? Maybe then he'll be happy to stay."

After some time, they eventually agreed to this, and Imam Abu Hanifa ﷺ then called the man back and said, "They're willing to return the money they took from you."

Seeing this as an opportunity to gain some extra money, the man replied, "I want *more* from them!"

Imam Abu Hanifa ﷺ asked, "Are you sure? What if the people you borrowed money from say to you, 'You have to repay me, and until you do, you can't leave the city.' Would that be more preferable to you?"

In defeat, the man finally said, "Please Hadrat, don't say this out loud. They might hear you and give me nothing." – *Lataaife-Ilmiyya Kitaabul-Azkiya, Pg. 142*

Lesson Through the help of Allah ﷻ, Imam Abu Hanifa ﷺ was able to solve the problems of people with great ease.

We also come to know that the dowry shouldn't be raised to the point that it's out of a person's reach (as this may bring unforeseen problems to the family).

20 – HIDDEN TREASURE

There was a man who once buried a portion of his wealth somewhere and later forgot where he put it. He sought advice from Imam Abu Hanifa ﷺ about this and was told, "Do nothing but read nafl Salaah tonight and you'll recall where you left it."

The man then proceeded home and decided to carry out this instruction. After only a few rakaats, he finally remembered where he'd left the money and decided that there was now no reason to continue, so he abandoned reading any more Salaah and fell off to sleep.

The next morning, he went to Imam Abu Hanifa ﷺ and said in happiness, "Imam! How did you know optional Salaah was the answer?!"

The great Imam replied, "I knew Shaitaan was going to remind you where you put it, because he wouldn't want you to spend your entire night reading nafl Salaah. It's only unfortunate that you didn't continue reading Salaah in gratitude to Allah ﷻ." – *Lataaife-Ilmiyya Kitaabul-Azkiya, Pg. 144, Jawaahirul-Bayaan, Pg. 96*

Lesson It's unfortunate that mankind only thinks of Allah ﷻ in times of need (whereas His remembrance is most treasured by Him in our daily lives).

21 – SON-IN-LAW

There was a man in the time of Imam Abu Hanifa ﷺ who used to harbour great enmity towards Hadrat Uthman ﷺ, going as far as calling him a Jew (Allah ﷻ forbid). The great Imam called the man to him and said, "I've found a very nice boy to marry your daughter. He has all the good qualities one can imagine. The only problem is he's a Jew."

The man replied, "You're such a prominent Imam and yet you think that it's permissible for a Jew to marry a Muslim?! I only know such a thing to be incorrect."

Imam Abu Hanifa ﷺ then said, "*Subhanallah!* Why would it be wrong? You consider Hadrat Uthman ﷺ to be a Jew, yet the Holy Prophet ﷺ gave *two* of his daughters to him!"

The man immediately realized his mistake, repented for having such evil thoughts against Hadrat Uthman ﷺ, and later became very wealthy due to the blessings he attained from Imam Abu Hanifa ﷺ. – *Tazkiratul-Auliya, Pg. 250*

Lesson Imam Abu Hanifa ﷺ and other Friends of Allah ﷺ throughout Islamic History have diverted many misled people to the straight path, which is why Allah ﷻ says in the Holy Quran, "كونوا مع الصادقين Be with the truthful." – *Surah Tauba (9), Verse 119*

We also come to know that having enmity towards Hadrat Uthman ؓ is in fact enmity towards the Holy Prophet ﷺ himself.

22 – HUSBAND & WIFE

A husband and wife once got into an argument, which prompted the husband to say, "Oath on Allah ﷻ, I'll never speak to you again until you speak to me first!"

His wife then retorted, "And oath on Allah ﷻ, I too will never speak to you again until you speak to me first!"

This put them in quite a predicament.

After some time, the husband decided to go to Imam Abu Hanifa ؓ to find a solution to the problem. The Imam explained, "You can speak to your wife, because after you said that you'll never speak to her again until she speaks to you, if she'd remained silent at that time, the oath would've been emplaced, but by her swearing her own oath thereafter, she said something to you in doing this, and so you're not liable to follow your oath anymore." – *Jawaahirul-Bayaan, Pg. 95*

23 – TRACKING THIEVES

A group of thieves once broke into a house at night and woke up the family within. In desperation, one of the robbers grabbed hold of the father and forced him to swear the following oath, "I give my wife three talaaqs if I tell anyone who the thieves are."

After that, they looted the entire house and ran away.

The next morning, the father saw the crooks walking around the city numerous times but didn't say anything (due to not wanting to be separated from his wife). He eventually decided to go to Imam Abu Hanifa ؓ to see if he could help him.

To solve this dilemma, the great Imam announced to the rich and prominent people of the area, "Help this poor man by gathering all the immoral and accused people of the city into one mansion."

He then turned to the father and said, "Now stand with me at the mansion door. As each person leaves, I'll ask you if he was one of the thieves or not. If he isn't, say "No"; but if he is, don't say anything, because remember, you'll be divorcing your wife if you tell me who the thieves are."

So, one-by-one, everyone inside was then told to leave the house, and in time, all the thieves were seized *without* the man having to divorce his wife!
– *Lataaife-Ilmiyya Kitaabul-Azkiya, Imam Ibn Jauzi ﷺ, Pg. 138*

24 – An 'Obedient' Army

An official of Khalifa Mansoor by the name of Rabee used to harbor great enmity towards Imam Abu Hanifa ﷺ. Once, when the Imam was present in the Khalifa's court after being summoned by him, Rabee said to the Khalifa, "Leader of the Faithful! Abu Hanifa goes against your grandfather, Hadrat Ibn Abbas ﷺ. Your grandfather said that after taking an oath, if 'Insha-Allah' (meaning, "If Allah ﷻ wills.") is said even one or two days later, it invalidates the oath, whereas Abu Hanifa ﷺ says that only when 'Insha-Allah' is said *with the oath* is the oath not emplaced. Otherwise, it stands."

Imam Abu Hanifa ﷺ replied, "Leader of the Faithful, Rabee wishes to diminish any obedience you have in your army."

The Khalifa enquired, "How so?"

Imam Abu Hanifa ﷺ explained, "Your army could simply swear that they will be obedient to you and then just go back to their homes and say 'If Allah ﷻ wills.'"

Hearing this, the Khalifa laughed and said, "Rabee! Don't annoy Abu Hanifa ﷺ."

As they walked out of the court, Rabee said to the great Imam, "Today you subjected me to disgrace."

The great Imam replied, "Because you did the same thing first." – *Lataaife-Ilmiyya Kitaabul-Azkiya, Pg. 140, Khairaatul-Hisaan, Pg. 101*

25 – Apt Reply

The respect shown to Imam Abu Hanifa ﷺ by the Khalifa Abu Ja'far Mansoor was of an unusually high standard, making the companion of the ruler (Abul-Abbas Tusi) very envious of him. Once, while in the Khalifa's court, Abul-Abbas Tusi asked the great Imam, "Abu Hanifa ﷺ! If the Khalifa orders us to kill a person without us knowing that the order is Haraam, would the killing be permissible?"

He replied, "Would the Khalifa order something that is wrong?"

Abul-Abbas Tusi answered, "Definitely not!"

Imam Abu Hanifa ⚮ then asked, "Then why would you hesitate in carrying out any order of his?"

Hearing this, the poor Abul-Abbas Tusi was unfortunately unable to respond. – *Khairaatul-Hisaan, Pg. 101*

Lesson In his time and even today, Imam Abu Hanifa ⚮ always had detractors, yet these people do nothing but ultimately bring humiliation unto themselves.

26 – PEACOCK THIEF

A man once had a peacock of his stolen by someone. He went to Imam Abu Hanifa ⚮ to complain about this and was told by him, "Don't say anything about this."

The great Imam then proceeded to the musjid and said to the congregation as they were getting ready for Salaah, "Doesn't the man who stole my neighbour's peacock have any shame? He's going to read Salaah while the colours of peacock feathers are still on his head!"

As soon he said this, someone in the crowd ducked to hide his face. Imam Abu Hanifa ⚮ spotted him and cried out, "You're the thief! Give it back to the man!"

As a result, the culprit could do nothing but retrieve the peacock and hand it back to its rightful owner. – *Khairaatul-Hisaan, Pg. 102*

Lesson Which thief could ever hide from one of the most learned men of his time?!

27 – FLOUR

Hadrat A'mash ⚮ was a renowned Commentator of Hadith with a short temper who lived in the time of Imam Abu Hanifa ⚮. Once, while quarrelling with his wife, he said to her, "You have three *talaaqs* from me the moment you say, write, send a message, tell someone else who'll tell me, or gesture that the flour in the house is finished!"

In this predicament, the wife of Hadrat A'mash ⚮ didn't know what to do and decided to meet with Imam Abu Hanifa ⚮ (after being guided by someone to do so). The Imam advised her, "When the flour's finished, tie the bag to your husband's clothes while he's asleep. He'll wake up and see it for himself."

The women did as she was told. And so, when her husband saw the flour tied to his clothes upon awakening, he said, "Oath on Allah ﷻ, this can only be the solution of Imam Abu Hanifa ⌾! While he's alive, how will I be successful? He disgraces us in front of our women and shows us how helpless and wrong we are in our decisions." – *Jawaahirul-Bayaan fi Tarjamatil-Khairaatil-Hisaan, Pg. 102*

Lesson Even eminent Commentators of Hadith (محدّثين) recognized the intellect and wisdom of Imam Abu Hanifa ⌾.

28 – A CUP OF WATER

A person in the time of Imam Abu Hanifa ⌾ once asked his wife to bring him a cup of water. As she approached him with it, he said to her out of some displeasure, "I'm not drinking it, and you have three talaaqs from me if you drink it, give it to someone else, or if it's poured out," in this way putting his wife in great distress.

When Imam Abu Hanifa ⌾ came to know of this vow, he said, "Put a piece of clothing in the cup to absorb the water and then leave it out in the sun to dry. In this way, the divorce will not be emplaced." – *Khairaatul-Hisaan, Pg. 104*

Lesson We again see the immense knowledge of Imam Abu Hanifa ⌾, who was able to solve even the most difficult of problems with ease. How then can people who don't even understand simple things in the field of academics hope to think that their deductions in Islamic Law are above those of the four great Imams?!

29 – CHICKEN EGG

A man once vowed to never eat a chicken's egg, only what he attained from the sleeve of his friend. When his friend took out what he had with him, the man unfortunately found that too to be a chicken's egg and had no idea what to do. He eventually sought advice from Imam Abu Hanifa ⌾ and was told, "Keep the egg incubated under a chicken. When it hatches, cook it whenever you wish and then eat it. The vow won't break." – *Khairaatul-Hisaan, Pg. 109*

Imam Abu Hanifa 🕮 once presented himself in Madina before the grandson of Hadrat Ali 🕮 (Hadrat Muhammad ibn Hasan 🕮), who said to him, "You're the Imam I've been hearing of, the one who chooses to follow his logic over the commands of my great-grandfather (i.e. the Holy Prophet 🕮)."

Imam Abu Hanifa 🕮 replied, "Allah 🕮 forbid! How could I do such a thing?! Sit with me for a while. You deserve respect just like the Prophet 🕮."

So, when Hadrat Muhammad ibn Hasan 🕮 decided to sit with him, the following conversation took place between them,

Imam Abu Hanifa 🕮 "Tell me, who is weaker between men and women?"

Hadrat Muhammad ibn Hasan 🕮 "Women."

Imam Abu Hanifa 🕮 "And in inheritance, who gets the bigger share?"

Hadrat Muhammad ibn Hasan 🕮 "Men"

Imam Abu Hanifa 🕮 "So, if I put my logic over Islamic commands, I should've said that *women* should get the bigger share of inheritance, not men, since women are the ones who are weaker.

"Now tell me, which is the greater form of worship, Salaah or fasting?"

Hadrat Muhammad ibn Hasan 🕮 "Salaah."

Imam Abu Hanifa 🕮 "And after giving birth, which of the two does a woman have to complete from whatever she missed?"

Hadrat Muhammad ibn Hasan 🕮 "Fasting."

Imam Abu Hanifa 🕮 "So, if I'd put my logic over the Hadith, I should've said that the *Salaah* that a pregnant woman missed should be fulfilled, not her fasts (since Salaah is the greater form of worship).

"Lastly, tell me, which is the dirtier of the two liquids, urine or semen?"

Hadrat Muhammad ibn Hasan ﷺ "Urine."

Imam Abu Hanifa ﷺ "If I'd put my logic over the Hadith, I should've said that Ghusl is compulsory after passing *urine*, not semen, since urine is dirtier."

Hearing this, Hadrat Muhammad ibn Hasan ﷺ then kissed the forehead of Imam Abu Hanifa ﷺ and said, "Now I know the things being said about you is just slander." – *Jawaahirul-Bayaan, Pg. 106*

Lesson We come to know that the accusations leveled against Imam Abu Hanifa ﷺ (that he placed his own judgments over the commands of Allah ﷻ & His Beloved Prophet ﷺ) are unjustified and incorrect. Indeed, the teachings of the great Saint were always in accordance with the one, true Islamic path.

31 – A POT OF GOLD

Once, just before a man could pass away, he gave a pot of 1,000 dinārs to a friend of his and said, "When my son grows up, give him whatever you want from this."

Years later, when his son reached the age of maturity, the man gave back the pot to him with nothing in it, and the son conveyed this to Imam Abu Hanifa ﷺ. The great Imam called the man to him and said, "Give this boy all of the 1,000 dinārs, because the order from his father was to give him '*whatever you want*' from it, and since you wanted all of it, that's the amount you have to give him."

So, the poor man had no option but to do as he was told. – *Jawaahirul-Bayaan, Pg. 108*

Lesson Islam emphasizes never going against a promise or stealing the wealth of an orphan.

32 – A BEDOUIN & SATTU

Imam Abu Hanifa ﷺ was once walking somewhere when he began to feel very thirsty. Seeing a Bedouin on the road with a water-bag in his possession, he asked him if he could have a sip from it and was told, "No! But I'll give you the entire bag for five dirhams."

The great Imam accepted this offer, gave him the money and took the water for himself. He then offered the Bedouin some *sattu* he had with him (which was immersed in olive-oil) and said, "You can eat from it as much as you wish."

Without hesitation, the Bedouin began to partake in it and continued until he was completely satisfied. He then felt thirsty and asked if he could have some of his previously-owned water. The great Imam replied, "No. I'll only give it to you for five dirhams, not less."

The poor man could then do nothing but return the five dirhams he took from him, leaving Imam Abu Hanifa ؓ with the same amount of money he had before, but now with some water to boot. – *Lataaife-Ilmiyya Kitaabul-Azkiya, Pg. 131*

Lesson Those who have been granted wisdom by Allah ﷻ use it to gain leverage over their problems.

33 – A Reply to Khārijees

During the mischief of the Khārijees, Imam Abu Hanifa ؓ was once captured by them and brought before their leader (Dihaak), who told the Imam to repent for not accepting their beliefs. The Imam replied, " انا تائب من كل كفر I make tauba from every form of infidelity," and was subsequently set free.

As he left, one of the Khārijee officials told Dihaak, "Abu Hanifa simply made tauba against all incorrect beliefs. He didn't necessarily say that he agreed to ours."

So, the great Imam was brought again to the gathering and was told, "Shaikh! I believe you have a problem with our beliefs. We accept orders only from the Quran, and take it alone to be the judge in our matters."

Seeing that he wasn't going to be left alone by these people any time soon, Imam Abu Hanifa ؓ then raised four objections against them from the Holy Quran before asking, "Is this what you *presume* I have done, or are you certain?"

Dihaak replied, "It's just an assumption."

Imam Abu Hanifa ؓ then read the verse of the Holy Quran,

إن بعض الظن إثم
"Some presumptions are sins."
– Surah Hujarāt (49), Verse 12

29

and argued, "You believe that every sin is an act of infidelity, so now *you* have to make tauba for presuming things."

Dihaak replied, "You're correct. I apologise."

Lesson Devious sects within Islam were always unable to divert the Friends of Allah ﷻ from the one, true Islamic path, which is why even until today, no Saint has emerged from any other sect besides the majority Ahle-Sunnah wal-Jamaah ('Sunni' Muslims).

34 – THE SECRET OF THE APPLE*

Once, while Imam Abu Hanifa ؓ was in the musjid with his students, a woman walked inside with a red and yellow apple in her hands and gave it to him without saying anything. Imam Abu Hanifa ؓ broke the apple into two pieces and handed it back to her, after which she was satisfied and then walked away.

Confused by this, the students asked him, "Imam, what was the secret of that apple?"

He replied, "She asked me a question and I answered it."

They then asked, "And what was the question?"

Imam Abu Hanifa ؓ answered, "She was trying to tell me that the blood that emerges from a woman is, like the apple, sometimes red and sometimes yellow, and she wanted to know if both were classified as blood in menstruation. By breaking the apple in two, I told her that until the blood is as white as the apple inside, the bleeding will *always* be classified as menstruation." – *Raudul-Faa'iq, Pg. 119*

Lesson In the earlier centuries, women showed great interest in Islam and were always keen to learn its laws so that they could be saved from living in sin – since on the Day of Judgment, ignorance will not be accepted as a valid excuse for one's crimes.

35 – THE PLAINS OF QIYAAMAT

Hadrat Naufal ibn Hayaan ؓ narrates, "After the demise of Imam Abu Hanifa ؓ, I had a dream in which I was present on the plains of Qiyaamat with everyone in creation there in wait to account for their deeds. I saw the Holy Prophet ﷺ at the Fountain of Kauthar with many illuminated people standing beside him. One man on his right had a very handsome face with a white head & beard and stood out amongst the rest.

"I then saw Imam Abu Hanifa ؓ near the Holy Prophet ﷺ and approached him. After making Salaam, I asked him if I could have some water from the Fountain and was told, "Until the Prophet ﷺ gives permission, I cannot do such a thing."

Rasoolullah ﷺ then said, "Give him some."

The Imam then poured some of it for me into a cup. After drinking it, I asked him, "Who's that old, handsome man to the right of Rasoolullah ﷺ?"

He replied, "That's Hadrat Ibrahim ؑ, and the man to his left is Hadrat Abu Bakr Siddique ؓ."

And, like that, I continued to ask questions and the great Imam continued to answer them. – *Tazkiratul-Auliya*

Lesson Imam Abu Hanifa ؓ has been shown to have received acceptance by the Holy Prophet ﷺ on many occasions and in different ways, and it's because of this guidance and special closeness he had with him that he could correctly simplify and streamline the thousands of Islamic laws for our ease.

36 – THE DREAM OF IMAM SHAFI ؓ

Imam Shafi ؓ narrates, "During my childhood, I had a dream in which I saw the Holy Prophet ﷺ asking me, "Boy, who are you?"

I replied, "O Rasoolullah ﷺ! I'm from your Ummah."

I then moved closer. When I was near him, he placed some of his blessed saliva in my mouth and said, "Go. You have been bestowed with the bounty and blessings of Allah ﷻ."

Immediately after that, Hadrat Ali ؓ appeared, removed the ring from his finger and placed it on mine." – *Tazkiratul-Auliya, Pg. 255*

Lesson With the blessings and support of Allah ﷻ, the Holy Prophet ﷺ and the Glorious Sahaabah ؓ, Imam Shafi ؓ became a light in the darkness of his era and greatly assisted the Ummah with his tremendous academic contributions.

37 – THE INTELLIGENCE OF A CHILD

The mother of Imam Shafi ؓ was a very pious woman of the Bani Hashim and was so trustworthy that people would keep their belongings with her for lengthy periods at a time.

Once, two men arrived at her door and entrusted a box to her. Some days later, one of them returned and asked for it. The mother of Imam Shafi ؤ thought nothing of this and handed it over to him.

A few more days later, the other man arrived and *also* requested the box. This time, however, Imam Shafi's ؤ mother could do nothing but explain, "I've already given it to your friend."
The man asked, "Didn't we tell you to only give the box back when both of us are here with you?!"
She sadly replied, "Yes…you did."
The man then angrily asked, "Then why did you give it to him?!"
The mother of Imam Shafi ؤ then began to get very worried and wondered what would happen now. At that very moment, Imam Shafi ؤ was returning from Madrassah and saw his mother in a troubled state. He asked her, "Why are you sad?"
She then related the entire incident to him, after which Imam Shafi ؤ replied, "Don't worry about this. Who's the man who wants the box?"
The man replied, "I am."
Imam Shafi ؤ then said, "You'll get the box back, but since we couldn't give it to your friend alone, how can we give it to you alone? You have to find your friend first and bring him here with you."
With nothing to say, the man then turned around and walked away. – *Tazkiratul-Auliya, Pg. 255*

Lesson Even in his childhood, Imam Shafi ؤ displayed immense wisdom. How then couldn't he have grown up to be such a great leader of the Ummah?

38 – ON THE KING'S THRONE

The Khalifa of his time, Haroon Rashid, was once having an argument with his wife when she said, "You're an inmate of Jahannam!"
Hearing this, the Khalifa replied, "If that's true, you have talaaq from me!"
Both then separated from one another in anger.

After some time, due to his intense love for his wife, Haroon Rashid summoned the Islamic Scholars to his court and requested them to help find a solution to this problem. None could give an answer and unanimously agreed that whether the Khalifa was a Jahannami or not was something only Allah ﷻ would know.

A small boy then stood up in the gathering and said, "With your permission, I'd like to give an answer."

The people were amused by this and thought, "When such eminent Scholars cannot find an answer to this, what could this boy possibly tell us?"

Nevertheless, Haroon Rashid called the boy towards him and said, "Tell us what you think."

The boy began, "First, tell me: do you need me, or do I need you?"

"I need you," said the Khalifa.

The boy then said, "Then descend from your throne and let me sit on it to answer you, because the rank of a scholar is elevated."

The Khalifa agreed to this, came down from his throne and allowed the boy to sit on it. The boy then asked him, "Now tell me, have you ever restrained yourself from a sin, even though you had the power to commit it, purely in the fear of Allah ﷻ?"

The Khalifa replied, "Oath on Allah ﷻ, I do such a thing!"

The boy then said, "Then the verdict is you are *not* an inmate of Jahannam, but an inmate of Paradise."

The Scholars asked him, "Where's your proof for this?"

The boy replied, "Allah ﷻ states in the Holy Quran,

وأما من خاف مقام ربه ونهى النفس عن الهوى ، فإن الجنة هي المأوى

"And for such as had entertained the fear of standing before their Lord's (tribunal) and had restrained (their) soul from lower desires, their abode will be the Garden."
– Surah Nazi'at (79), Verses 40-1

Hearing this, everyone began to praise the boy and said, "For someone who shows such intellect and wisdom at such a young age, how magnificent will he be in his prime?!"

(And who was this boy in the court of the Khalifa? It was none other than the celebrated Imam Shafi ﵁). – *Tazkiratul-Auliya, Pg. 256*

39 – PRIESTS

The King of Rome used to send some money annually to the Leader of the Muslims, Haroon Rashid. One year, he sent some priests instead and relayed the following message to him, "If your scholars debate with my priests and are victorious over them, I'll continue sending money to you."

After accepting the challenge, Haroon Rashid gathered the Islamic Scholars of his area on the banks of the Tigris River and told the priests that the challenge would be carried out there. He also saw Imam Shafi ﷺ in the crowd and decided to seek help from him specifically, saying to him, "Imam, you speak to them."

In reply, Imam Shafi ﷺ grabbed his *musalla*, spread it over the water of the Tigris River and sat on it, saying, "Whoever from the priests wants to discuss anything, he must come here and speak to me."

Seeing this, the *entire gathering* of priests became Muslims on the hands of the great Imam!

When the King of Rome was informed of this, he replied, "We're lucky that that Imam didn't come here, otherwise everyone in Rome would've become Muslim." – *Tazkiratul-Auliya, Pg. 258*

Lesson After witnessing their eminence and authority, many groups of people throughout history became Muslims on the hands of the Saints.

40 – INTUITION

Imam Shafi ﷺ and Imam Ahmad ﷺ were once sitting together in the musjid when a man entered it and began to read Salaah.

Imam Ahmad ﷺ looked at him and said, "This man's a blacksmith."

Imam Shafi ﷺ replied, "No, he's a wood-gatherer."

After the man completed his Salaah, he was asked what he was and said, "I *was* a blacksmith last year, but now I gather wood for a living." – *Nuzhatul-Majaalis, Vol. 1, Pg. 117*

Lesson Whatever emerges from the mouth of a friend of Allah ﷻ is the truth.

41 – INHERITANCE OF THE PROPHETS

A Friend of Allah ﷻ (Hadrat Rabee ﷺ) once had a dream in which he saw a group of people carrying the blessed *janaazah* of Hadrat Adam ﷺ. He immediately awoke and then proceeded to a dream-interpreter to know of its meaning.

The interpreter replied, "It means a great Scholar of our time will soon leave us, because the unique knowledge of Hadrat Adam ﷺ has been expressed in the Quran,

وعلم آدم الأسماء كلها
"And He taught Adam ﷺ the nature of all things."
– Surah Baqarah (2), Verse 31

Accordingly, a few days later, people were saddened to hear that the demise of Imam Shafi ؓ had occurred. – *Tazkiratul-Auliya, Pg. 259*

Lesson The Four Imams are the successors to the Prophets and received great honour in their lifetimes because of this.

We also come to know that Imam Shafi ؓ is accepted as a major Scholar in Islamic History.

42 – IMAM AHMAD IBN HAMBAL ؓ

In Baghdad, during the rise of the Mu'tazila mischief, some people wanted to force Imam Ahmad ibn Hambal ؓ to say that the Quran is a creation of Allah ﷻ [as opposed to the belief of the Muslim Ummah that the Quran is the *speech* of Allah ﷻ, and therefore His quality].

So, after a number of plots against him, the great Imam was eventually seized and taken to the oppressive Khalifa of the time. As he entered his court, a constable standing at the doorway said to him, "O Leader of the Muslims! Don't call the Quran a creation, but remain silent like the dead. See, I was once accused of theft and was caned 1,000 times for it, but I *insisted* that I did not steal the item. Eventually, I was freed…even though I had been lying all that time! So, if someone like me can be successful through dishonesty, how can you not gain success when you are on the path of truth?"

Imam Ahmad ؓ was extremely affected by these words and replied, "*Jazakallah* (May Allah ﷻ reward you), I'll remember these words of yours and never forsake the truth."

The Imam was then taken into the court and forced to say that the Quran is a creation of Allah ﷻ, but he refused to do so (even after being tied to a wall and lashed countless times afterwards).

As he was being whipped, his lower-garment began to loosen and fall off, but with his hands restrained, the Imam could unfortunately do nothing about it. The people who were witnessing this then noticed an unseen force re-tying the garment for him. Seeing this miracle of his, the great Imam was then set free. – *Tazkiratul-Auliya, Pg. 261*

Lesson Imam Ahmad ibn Hambal ﷺ was the Leader of the Muslims and a staunch campaigner of the truth. Even with all the slander and problems his enemies threw his way, he never forsook the one, true Islamic path.

We also learn that the Four Imams were so respectful of the Holy Quran that they were even willing to be whipped and tortured in upholding the respect of it.

43 – RESPECT & ITS REWARD

Imam Ahmad ibn Hambal ﷺ was once making wudhu on the edge of a stream next to another man (who was also making wudhu) upstream. When the man saw Imam Ahmad ibn Hambal ﷺ, he walked down, passed the great Imam and continued making wudhu below him in respect.

After his demise, someone saw the man in a dream and asked him, "What did you receive from Allah ﷻ?"

He replied, "Allah ﷻ showed me mercy and granted me salvation for what I did when Imam Ahmad ﷺ was making wudhu." – *Tazkiratul-Auliya, Pg. 262*

Lesson Allah ﷻ is pleased when one shows respect to His Friends and is displeased when one shows enmity. For this reason, we should always fear doing anything showing disrespect to the Saints (and earn their anger as a result).

44 – KNOWLEDGE & PRACTICE

A student of Imam Ahmad ibn Hambal ﷺ once stayed the night in his house. In the morning, the Imam noticed that the pot of water he'd left for him during the night hadn't been touched, so he asked him, "Why didn't you use the water?"

The student replied, "Hadrat, what would I need water for?"

Imam Ahmad ibn Hambal ﷺ answered, "Use it to make wudhu and spend the night in worship. Otherwise, why are you learning?" – *Tazkiratul-Auliya, Pg. 364*

Lesson Without practice, there is no benefit in acquiring knowledge.

The son of Imam Ahmad ibn Hambal 🙵 (Hadrat Salih 🙵) was the judge of Asfahaan and would fast every day and read optional Salaah every night. One day, a servant of the Imam attained some yeast from his son's home and prepared his bread with it. When it was brought before him, Imam Ahmad ibn Hambal 🙵 asked him, "What's in this bread that made it rise like this?"

The servant replied, "Hadrat, I took some yeast from your son's kitchen and mixed it into your flour."

Imam Ahmad 🙵 then said, "He's the judge of Asfahaan, so I'm not worthy to eat this. What must I do with it now?"

He then instructed, "If any beggar comes, give it to him and say that the yeast is from Salih 🙵 and the flour is from Ahmad ibn Hambal 🙵. Otherwise, you may take it for yourself if you wish." – *Tazkiratul-Auliya, Pg. 263*

Lesson The Friends of Allah 🙼 are extremely cautious when treading on doubt. How sad is it, then, that today we don't even care about committing sins *openly*?

46 – A MOUNTAIN MADE OF GOLD

Imam Ahmad ibn Hambal 🙵 was once walking somewhere when he got lost and forgot which way to go. He decided to ask a man sitting in a corner nearby, but the man simply saw him and began to weep.

Imam Ahmad ibn Hambal 🙵 thought, "Perhaps he's crying because he's hungry," and he then offered him a piece of bread.

The man became angry with this and said, "Ahmad ibn Hambal 🙵! Who are you to try and get between me and my Lord?! Are you unsatisfied with the work of Allah 🙼?! Maybe that's why you lost your way!"

These words had a great effect on the Imam. He then thought, "O Allah 🙼! Are there such Friends of Yours hidden in places like these?!"

The man replied, "O Ahmad 🙵, what are you saying?! There are servants of Allah 🙼 who, after swearing by Him, are able to turn the roads and mountains in their path into gold!"

Indeed, Imam Ahmad ibn Hambal 🙵 then noticed that everything around him seemed to begin turning into gold before his very eyes. He then heard a voice from the unseen say, "O Ahmad 🙵! This is such a person that We would turn the Heavens and the Earth upside-down for his sake!" – *Tazkiratul-Auliya*

Lesson The Saints are so elevated within creation that they know the secrets of one's heart and can turn mountains into gold simply on their command. If this is the authority of just the *Friends* of Allah ﷻ, what could possibly be the authority of our Prophet ﷺ, the very *Beloved* of Allah ﷻ?!

47 – THE DREAM OF IBN KHUZAIMAH ﷺ

After the demise of Imam Ahmad ibn Hambal ﷺ, a Saint by the name of Hadrat Muhammad ibn Khuzaimah ﷺ saw him in a dream walking somewhere and asked, "Where are you going?"
The great Imam replied, "To the House of Peace."

"What did Allah ﷻ grant you?"

"He forgave me, then He had a crown placed on my head and shoes put on my feet before saying, "You are being granted all of this due to not saying that the Quran is a creation." – *Tazkiratul-Auliya, Pg. 267*

Lesson For his selfless service to the deen, Imam Ahmad ibn Hambal ﷺ was bestowed great honour in the Hereafter.

48 – IMAM MALIK ﷺ

Hadrat Muhammad ibn Abis-Saraa Asqalaani ﷺ once saw the Holy Prophet ﷺ in a dream and asked him, "O Rasoolullah ﷺ, tell me something that I may relate to others on your behalf."
He replied, "Asqalaani ﷺ, I bestowed Anas ibn Malik ﷺ with a treasure which he is currently distributing amongst you. That treasure is his book, *Muatta*." – *Raudul-Faa'iq, Pg. 148*

Lesson The eminence of Imam Malik ﷺ has been acknowledged by the Holy Prophet ﷺ himself, and his compilation, 'Muatta', is both sound and referred to as a treasure by him.

The Khalifa of his time, Haroon Rashid, was once present in Madina when he heard that Imam Malik ﷺ was also in the city teaching his book, 'Muatta', to the people. He sent a message to the Imam requesting him to come and deliver these lectures directly to him, but the Imam refused to do so and replied, "Tell Haroon Rashid that knowledge doesn't go to a person. A seeker of something goes to *it*."

So, the Khalifa proceeded to the Imam's gathering, sat next to him (on his request) and said, "Read your Muatta while I listen to it."

Imam Malik ﷺ replied, "I've never taught like this. Others read in my class while I listen to them."

"Fine, then tell everyone to leave so that I may read to you alone."

Imam Malik ﷺ was still dissatisfied and said, "When knowledge is kept from the people for only a specific few, it brings no benefit with it."

So, the Khalifa had no option but to begin reading while everyone sat and listened to him.

The great Imam then advised Haroon Rashid, "Humility is necessary in attaining knowledge. Come down from your platform and continue reading in front of me."

And so, the Khalifa descended and sat level with the class before continuing. – *Raudul-Faa'iq, Pg. 148*

Lesson As stated, humility is necessary in the acquisition of knowledge.

We also come to know that the previous kings showed great interest in learning about Islam and were deeply respectful of the Quran & Hadith.

50 – A SCORPION'S STING

Imam Malik ﷺ was once teaching the narrations of the Holy Prophet ﷺ when his students noticed that his face was slowly turning yellow and beginning to show great discomfort. Nevertheless, the great Imam continued until the lesson was over.

When he was later asked about this, he lifted up his garment to show a scorpion (which had stung him six times) and said, "This scorpion was stinging me but I continued the lesson out of respect for the Hadith. Whoever I may be, the narrations of the Prophet ﷺ are more important."
– *Raudul-Faa'iq, Pg. 149*

Lesson The Imams showed great reverence to the words of the Holy Prophet ﷺ, which is something we should also try to adopt within ourselves today.

51 – DEMISE

Imam Shafi ﷺ states, "While in Makkah, my aunt once had a dream in which she saw someone saying, 'The demise of the greatest Scholar of our time has come to pass!'"

It was on that very day that we came to know of the demise of Imam Malik ﷺ." انا لله و انا اليه راجعون.

Lesson Imam Malik ﷺ was a great Scholar and was, for this reason, accepted amongst the Four Imams ﷺ.

52 – THE JEWELLERY MERCHANT

Hadrat Hasan Basri ﷺ was a merchant of pearls and jewellery in the early part of his life. Selling all types, he would occasionly present some as gifts to the major kings of the time and once went (for this reason) to the Caesar of Rome. Upon his arrival, he met with one of the Caesar's ministers and told him why he'd come. The minister replied, "The Caesar has very important work, so there'll be no opportunity to see him."

When Hadrat Hasan Basri ﷺ insisted that he see him, the minister took him to a field where a magnificent gold tent was assembled, and around which lay a velvet carpet (the best of its kind). Even its poles were made of silver. The minister placed Hadrat Hasan ﷺ behind a screen wherefrom he could witness what was happening inside. He noticed that the tent was actually assembled over the grave of the king's son, and that today was the annual gathering stipulated in his honour.

A group of Christians was seen walking inside, reciting something and then leaving crying. A group of doctors and intellectuals then entered and did the same thing. Then a massive army with their swords, and finally a group of young, attractive women with open hair holding trays made of gold full of pearls and jewels. After circling the grave, they too began crying (before exiting the tent).

After this, the Caesar of Rome himself walked in, stood at his son's grave and said, "Son. You are so beloved to me, but unfortunately your demise has come to pass. If the One Who took your life would return it in exchange for the recitals of priests, then I have priests here with me, but I know it will be of no benefit. If I knew that He'd bring you back to life through the treatment of doctors and experts, then I have such people here with me as well, but I know that He is far more superior and that these doctors will be of no benefit. O Son, if the One Who took you away from me would be scared of a great army, then I also have such an army here with me, but I know He will not be intimidated. And if He wanted women and the treasures of the world, then I even have both here with me, but I know He doesn't ask for them. He will never give you back to us, and for this, I seek your permission to leave you like this for another year."

The Caesar then turned around and walked away.

After witnessing this, the love for the world in Hadrat Hasan Basri ﷺ shattered, and he then abandoned the selling of worldly treasures for the purchasing of Heavenly ones, preparing himself for his destination to the Hereafter. He later returned to Basra, swore to himself that he would forsake the laughter of this world, and began to engross himself so much in worship that no individual could equal him. (For 70 years, he was distinctively known to have always been with wudhu, even until his last breath). – *Tazkiratul-Auliya*

Lesson Nothing [and no-one] in this world will save one from the Angel of Death ﷺ, let alone Allah ﷺ. Rich or poor, king or servant, all are equal in death and will have nothing to assist them in the Hereafter except piety.

53 – A LECTURE AMONGST JINNS

Hadrat Abdullah ﷺ narrates, "I once woke up early to perform Salaah with jama'ah and headed to the musjid of Hadrat Hasan Basri ﷺ. The musjid was closed when I got there, but I could hear Hadrat making dua inside while others were saying, "Ameen." I thought that this may have been his followers and decided to wait outside.

Later, I placed my hand on the door and it swung open. I walked in and saw no-one inside except Hadrat Hasan Basri ﷺ, so I read my Salaah in amazement and then asked him, "By Allah ﷺ, tell me who was with you saying 'Ameen' just now!"

He replied, "Don't tell anyone, but I have specified the night of every Jumaa to lecture to Jinns. They come and I speak in-front of them every week. When I'm done, I make dua and they say, 'Ameen.'" – *Tazkiratul-Auliya, Pg. 36*

Lesson The Friends of Allah ﷻ are so elevated within creation that even Jinns become their servants! We also come to know that specifying a time to perform a good deed (be it at night or day) is not a bad innovation, but permissible.

54 – THE OLD MAN IN MUSJID KHAEF*

Abu Amr was a hafiz in Basra who used to teach the Holy Quran. Once, a very young and handsome boy came to him and said, "Teach me the Quran too."

After looking at him inappropriately, Abu Amr and immediately realized that he'd forgotten the entire Quran!

Stunned, he proceeded to Hadrat Hasan Basri ﷺ and requested him to make dua for him. The great Saint replied, "The time of Hajj is close. Perform it and go to Musjid Khaef. There you'll see an old man sitting at the mihraab. Serve him if you must and don't waste his time. When he finishes his reading, go up to him, tell him what you need and request him to make dua for you."

Abu Amr did as he was told. And so, after performing Hajj, he proceeded to Musjid Khaef and indeed found an old man (whose appearance was full of noor and vigour) sitting at the mihraab, but since there were some other people around him, he sat and waited for them to finish first.

During this time, another man with brilliantly white and clean clothes entered the musjid. Those who were sitting got up to meet and speak to him for a while. When the time of Salaah approached, the man walked away (followed by everyone else). This left Abu Amr alone with the old man, and so he moved forward to sit closer to him.

When the man finally got up, Abu Amr greeted him and told him what had happened, at the same time crying and pleading for his assistance in becoming a hafiz again. The man looked at him sorrowfully and lifted his head to the sky. Before he could even lower it, the entire Quran returned to the memory of Abu Amr (!) after which he fell to the feet of the old man in joy!

The man then asked him, "Who told you about me?"

Abu Amr replied, "Hadrat Hasan Basri ﷺ."

The man then said, "*He* told you?! For humiliating me and revealing my secret, I'll humiliate him and reveal his secret! Did you see that man who came here at Zohr time with clean white clothes?"

Abu Amr replied, "Yes, I remember him."

The man continued, *"That* was Hasan Basri 🌸. He reads Zohr in Basra every day and then comes here to talk to us until Asr. When a person has someone like Hasan Basri 🌸 as his Imam, what dua does he need from us?!" – *Tazkiratul-Auliya, Pg. 38*

Lesson Those who seek assistance from the Friends of Allah 🌸 in times of need and request dua from them will surely have their difficulty alleviated.
   We also learn that major difficulties emerge from wicked glaring,

لان العلم نور من الله ، و نور الله لا يعطى لعاصى

'Because knowledge is Noor from Allah 🌺*,*
And the Noor of Allah 🌺 *isn't given to sinners.'*

Also, we see that the Friends of Allah 🌸 hide their excellences and choose to be humble in spite of their status. They don't think of themselves as greater than other Saints...but that others are greater than them.
   Lastly, we learn that the Friends of Allah 🌸 can travel hundreds of miles in a matter of moments. How then can ordinary people like us think of ourselves as equal to them when we can only travel as fast as modern transport permits?

55 – THE FIRE-WORSHIPPER SHAM'OON

There was a fireworshipper living next to Hadrat Hasan Basri 🌸 named Sham'oon who once fell sick. When news of this reached the great Saint, he decided to go and visit him.
   After entering Sham'oon's house, Hadrat Hasan 🌸 saw a fire burning and said, "Sham'oon, fear Allah 🌺 and become a Muslim. You've been worshipping this fire and smoke your entire life, now consider Islam. Maybe Allah 🌺 will forgive you for this."
   Sham'oon replied, "Show me the truth of Islam."
   Hadrat Hasan Basri 🌸 then said, "You've worshipped fire for seventy years while I haven't even once. Let's both put our hands in it and see whose hand it burns and whose it doesn't. It *should* forsake yours because you've been worshipping it all these years, but I have faith in Allah 🌺 that it won't burn me if I do it to show you His power against the weakness of this fire."
   He then placed his hand in the fire and left it inside for some time. When Sham'oon saw that the fire indeed had no effect on the great Saint, he

became uneasy and asked him, "How much can I worship Allah ﷻ now with the little time I have left?"

Hadrat Hasan Basri ؓ replied, "Don't think like that. Read the Kalima of Islam and you'll immediately gain His pleasure and will be forgiven for all you've done in the past."

Sham'oon said, "I'll believe in Allah ﷻ if you write some sort of contract that I won't be punished."

So, Hadrat Hasan Basri ؓ wrote out such a contract and handed it over, after which Sham'oon read the Kalima and entered Islam, saying, "When I die, give me ghusl and place this contract in my hand so that I may use it to escape any punishment in the Hereafter."

He then read the Kalima of Islam again and passed away.

As instructed, Hadrat Hasan Basri ؓ carried out his ghusl and read the Janaazah Salaah (with many people in attendance).

At night, he found it hard to sleep and stayed awake reading Salaah thinking, "I don't even have control over my own things. How could I have written such a contract over something in *Allah's* ﷻ control?!"

After eventually falling off to sleep, he saw Sham'oon in a dream walking in the gardens of Jannah wearing beautiful clothes with a crown on his head and asked him, "Sham'oon, what happened to you?"

Sham'oon replied, "Allah ﷻ showed me great favour and left me in a good place. He even permitted you to see me. Everything else I've been given cannot be explained. O Hasan ؓ, you've completed your obligation to me. Your contract came in handy, but now you may have it since I don't need it anymore."

Hadrat Hasan Basri ؓ then woke up and found the contract lying in his hand. – *Tazkiratul-Auliya, Pg. 39-40*

Lesson The Friends of Allah ؓ can turn even the staunchest of disbelievers towards Islam.

We also see that Allah ﷻ fulfils whatever His Friends ؓ promise to save them from being branded as liars.

56 – ALONG THE TIGRIS RIVER

Hadrat Hasan Basri ؓ was once walking along a riverbank when he noticed an Abyssinian lying down with a woman, drinking out of a bottle with her. He thought to himself, "I'm better than him because I'd never do something like that. There he is sitting with that woman drinking alcohol and leaving the bottle right in front of them (for everyone to see)."

At that moment, a ship filled with goods came towards them and began to sink. There were ten men on-board and all began to shout for their lives.

Seeing this, the Abyssinian jumped into the river and swam back with one person each time. After saving nine of them, he looked at Hadrat Hasan Basri ﷺ and said, "O Hasan ﷺ! Man of perfection! If you are better than me, save the tenth one! O Imam of the Muslims! It isn't nice to think badly of others! This woman is my mother, and in this bottle is water!"

Hearing this, Hadrat Hasan Basri ﷺ fell to the Abyssinian's feet and sought his forgiveness. – *Tazkiratul-Auliya, Pg. 40*

Lesson Unless one is *certain* of the truth, he shouldn't assume things.

We also come to know that even our innermost thoughts are not hidden from the Friends of Allah ﷺ.

57 – A BACKBITER'S REIMBURSEMENT

Someone once came to Hadrat Hasan Basri ﷺ and told him that a certain person had spoken ill of him. Hearing this, he called for some dry dates, set it on a plate and sent the dish to the person as a gift with the following message, "I cannot thank you enough. By backbiting against me, you've transferred the good acts from your Book of Deeds into mine. Since I can never repay you in full, I humbly ask of you to accept this minor gift from me."

When this reached its recipient, he was so overcome by the character of Hadrat Hasan Basri ﷺ (and ashamed of what he'd done) that he presented himself in front of the great Imam and sought his forgiveness! – *Tazkiratul-Auliya, Pg. 41*

Lesson The one who backbites is truly at fault (even if what he's saying is correct), and those that he speaks about gain benefit from his utterances and even receive his good deeds. Due to this, backbiting should be seriously refrained from.

We also learn that the Friends of Allah ﷺ don't commit bad in exchange for bad. Even if something cruel is done to them, they repay that person with good.

Hadrat Malik ibn Deenar ﷺ was once having a debate with an atheist. They continued to disagree with each other until it was finally decided that each should tie one of their hands to the other's and place both in a fire. The person whose hand didn't burn would be regarded as the truthful one, and the one whose hand burned would be the liar.

However, when they did this, it was the power of Allah ﷻ that the fire became cool for *both* of them and none of the hands burned!

This troubled Hadrat Malik ibn Deenar ﷺ immensely. He therefore went into sajda and implored, "O Allah ﷻ, what's happened here?!"

A voice was then heard saying, "Malik, the hand of the atheist was *tied to yours* and placed into the fire, and whatever is tied to you won't ever burn. If the atheist's hand was truly saved, it was only due to the blessings of *your hand*. You two should place your hands *separately* into the fire and then see the result."

So, when both decided to place their hands *individually* into the fire, the hand of Hadrat Malik ibn Deenar ﷺ was saved while the atheist's hand was burned! From this, it became known that he was the liar! – *Tazkiratul-Auliya, Pg. 50*

Lesson From the blessings of being with the Friends of Allah ﷺ and placing our hands in theirs, even sinful people are liberated from punishment. On the other hand, one gains nothing but loss and deficiencies when he separates himself from the Saints. This is why Allah ﷻ states in the Holy Quran, "كونوا مع الصادقين Be with the truthful[1]," and Maulana Jalaaluddin Rumi ﷺ writes, "صحبت صالح ترا صالح كند By being with the pious, one becomes pious."

59 – A JEWISH MAN'S DRAINPIPE

Hadrat Malik ibn Deenar ﷺ once rented a place next to a Jewish man whose door was close to his room. One day, the man fixed a drainpipe leading out of his house which would deposit some of its dirt directly into the house of Hadrat Malik ibn Deenar ﷺ. This continued for a while...but Hadrat Malik ibn Deenar ﷺ said nothing about it.

After some time, the Jewish man asked him, "Sir, has my drain been troubling you?"

The Saint replied, "It does, but I've left a bucket and broom nearby and clean whatever falls from it."

The man then asked, "Why do you trouble yourself? Why didn't you get angry about it?"

Hadrat Malik ibn Deenar ﷺ answered, "My Lord states in the Quran that those who suppress their anger and forgive others are indeed good people."

The man then said, "Then teach me the Kalima of Islam, for the religion that teaches such good can only be good itself." – *Tazkiratul-Auliya, Pg. 52*

Lesson Kindness is the nature of the eminent servants of Allah ﷻ. They don't get angry over the mistakes of people, but choose to forgive them instead.

We also come to know that Islam spreads through kindness and good character.

60 – HADRAT HABIB AJMI ﷺ

Hadrat Habib Ajmi ﷺ was a very wealthy man in the early stages of his life and used to loan out money to the people of Basra on interest. Every day he'd go out and harass them for his due amount, and when they simply couldn't give him any more, he'd say, "Fine, then give me something in exchange for coming here."

This is how he'd make ends meet.

One day, he went to one of his debtors and found no-one there except his wife. She explained, "My husband isn't here and I have nothing, but I did slaughter a sheep today and I still have its head. You can take it if you want."

Habib Ajmi ﷺ replied, "Give it to me."

He then proceeded to his house and said to his wife, "I received this sheep's head through interest and I want you to cook it."

His wife replied that there was neither bread nor firewood in the house.

"I'll go and get some from others," he answered, and when he came back, she began to cook it in a pot.

Before she could serve it, a beggar arrived at the door and asked for something for the sake of Allah ﷻ. Habib Ajmi ﷺ replied, "Go away! If I give you what I have, I'll have nothing for myself, and then *I'll* be the beggar!"

Hearing this, the beggar turned around and left.

When the wife of Habib Ajmi ♦ looked again in the pot, she was shocked to see nothing but blood inside and showed it to her husband, crying, "See what your immorality and miserliness has brought us!"

This brought a change of heart in Hadrat Habib Ajmi ♦. So, he immediately decided to mend his ways and said, "Be my witness that today I am repenting from every bad action."

He then went out to his debtors to retrieve his money and cancel the remaining interest emplaced on them.

It was the day of Jumaa and some children were playing about. When they saw Habib Ajmi ♦ walking towards them, they said amongst themselves, "Move out of the way! If the dirt from the shoes of that interest-dealer comes on us, we might turn out evil like him!"

Habib Ajmi ♦ was greatly saddened by this and thereafter decided to acquire help from Hadrat Hasan Basri ♦.

When he met him, he was told to make tauba to Allah ﷻ and was given some advice. After their conversation, Habib Ajmi ♦ experienced a revolution in his life and left the great Saint a beloved of Allah ﷻ himself!

As he proceeded back to his house, one of his debtors saw him and began to run away. Hadrat Habib Ajmi ♦ shouted, "Brother! Don't run from me! It's me who should be running from you!"

He then came across the boy who'd insulted him earlier – but this time, the boy saw him and said to his friends, "Move out of the way! Habib ♦ is coming after having repented. If our sand falls on him, we may be taken as sinners!"

Hearing this, Hadrat Habib Ajmi ♦ thought, "O Allah ﷻ, how amazing is Your mercy, that it was just today that I made tauba, yet You've already placed its effect in the heart of Your creation and made my name famous amongst them."

He then shouted, "Whoever gave anything to Habib (as interest) should come and take it back."

Hearing this, everyone who was in debt to Hadrat Habib Ajmi ♦ gathered around him, and all the wealth that he'd acquired was returned until nothing remained. – *Tazkiratul-Auliya, Pg. 59*

Lesson The mercy of Allah ﷻ is expansive, and those hearts which sincerely wish to repent from their sins are immediately embraced by it.

We also come to know that when someone loves Allah ﷻ, (وضع له القبول فى الارض) Allah ﷻ places the love of him into His entire creation.

The father of Sayyidah Rabia Basri ؓ was a very poor man with three daughters to look after. On the night Rabia Basri ؓ was born ('Rabia' meaning *fourth*), he had no money to buy anything and fell asleep in this worried state.

In his dream, the Holy Prophet ﷺ met with him and said, "Don't be sad. This girl will be a great and popular Saint. Go to the King of Basra tomorrow and deliver this message to him on a piece of paper on behalf of me:

'You read Durood Sharif on me 100 times a day and 400 on every night of Jumaa, but on the last night you forgot and didn't read anything. In compensation for this, give this man 400 dinaars.'

When the father of Rabia Basri ؓ awoke, he got up crying and proceeded to deliver this message to the king – giving it to one of the king's servants outside the palace and standing in wait there for his reply.

After the king read it, he cried tears of joy (knowing that the Holy Prophet ﷺ had remembered him) and ordered for 10,000 dinaars to be distributed amongst the poor. He also ordered for 400 dinaars to be given to the man who brought the message to him and requested that he come inside. However, before the order was carried out, the king *himself* stood up and said, "No, it would be disrespectful if I call him to me. I'd rather present myself in his service, and I'll clean his pathway with my beard if I have to!"

He then exited the palace, kissed the hand of Sayyidah Rabia Basri's ؓ father and respectfully said to him, "By Allah ﷻ! If you ever need anything from now onwards, please request it from me."

Lesson Sayyidah Rabia Basri ؓ was such a great and popular Saint that her eminence was mentioned even by the Holy Prophet ﷺ.

We also come to know two things: that the houses that include the pious servants of Allah ﷻ have continuous mercy and blessings showered upon them, and that the Prophet ﷺ is aware of the state of the Muslims and still assists them.

Durood Sharif is also shown here to bring great benefit to its reader; and not only is the Prophet ﷺ aware of those who read it, he even knows how much! Indeed, nothing concerning his Ummah is hidden from him.

62 – THE THIEF

Sayyidah Rabia Basri ؓ was once reading Salaah continuously and eventually fell asleep in tiredness.

That night, a thief broke into her house with the intention of grabbing her belongings and running away with it. However, as soon as he touched her bag, he immediately lost his vision!

In this worried state, he let go of the bag and was able to see again, but after picking it up a second time, he lost his eyesight once again! This happened two or three more times until he finally heard a voice from the unseen saying, "Fool! One friend sleeps but the Other is awake. When Rabia ؓ entrusted herself to Us, Shaitaan *himself* lost his power to go near her. So, what chance does an ordinary thief have of reaching *even her belongings*?! Go away!"

Hearing this, the thief immediately ran away. – *Tazkiratul-Auliya, Pg. 77*

63 – THE KING OF BALKH

Hadrat Ibrahim ibn Ad'ham ؓ was initially the king of Balkh and reigned with great majesty. (He used to be accompanied by forty soldiers armed with gold maces & shields behind and in front of him whenever he traveled.)

Once, while he was asleep, he heard footsteps on his roof and asked, "Who's there?"

A voice replied, "I'm looking for my camel."

The king answered in surprise, "Idiot! Why would you hope to find a camel on a roof?!"

The voice then said, "And what about you, negligent king? Why would you hope to find Allah ﷻ while wearing satin clothes and sitting on a throne? Isn't that more strange than trying to find a camel on a roof?"

Hadrat Ibrahim ibn Ad'ham ؓ was very affected by these words. Nevertheless, he fell off to sleep again.

The following day, he was sitting on his throne (in front of an audience) when a man full of splendour walked in his court and said, "I don't like this hotel."

The king was amused by this and replied, "This isn't a hotel. It's my palace."

The man then asked, "And who was here before you?"

"My father."

"And before him?"

"My grandfather."

"And before him?"

My great-grandfather."

The man then said, "So think, O king! No one stays here forever. What else could this be but a hotel?"

He then turned around and walked away. As he left, Hadrat Ibrahim ﷺ descended from his throne, ran towards him and asked, "Who are you?"

The individual replied, "I'm Khidr ﷺ."

This had a tremendous effect on Hadrat Ibrahim ibn Ad'ham ﷺ, and in time, he eventually abandoned his kingship and spent nine years in a cave engrossed in the worship of Allah ﷻ to eventually become the famous Saint he is known as today. – *Tazkiratul-Auliya*

Maulana Rumi ﷺ adds: Some time later, Hadrat Ibrahim ibn Ad'ham ﷺ was seen sitting near a river mending his clothes by a governor of the time. The governor thought to himself, "What did he attain by leaving his kingship to live like such a pauper?"

Hadrat Ibrahim ﷺ immediately threw his needle into the river and shouted, "Give my needle back!"

Thousands of fish then emerged above the surface, each with a gold needle in their mouths presenting it to the great Saint, but he simply looked at them and said, "I want my original one."

A small fish then emerged and placed it in front of him.

Hadrat Ibrahim ﷺ then looked at the governor and asked him, "Which government would you prefer to be king of *now*?"

Lesson It's extremely difficult to reach Allah ﷻ while surrounded by the splendour and riches of the world, which is why many Saints choose to live in isolation and therefore be able to concentrate more on attaining a special closeness to Him through undisrupted worship and reflection.

64 – THE SOUR POMEGRANATES

After abandoning his kingship, Hadrat Ibrahim ibn Ad'ham ﷺ was once temporarily entrusted to look after a garden for someone and worked in it as a servant.

One day, the owner of the garden (not knowing who he was) said to him, "Fetch me a sweet pomegranate."

Hadrat Ibrahim ibn Ad'ham ؇ left the area, broke a pomegranate off a tree and returned to give it to him. When the owner tasted it, he found it to be sour and said, "Get me another one."

After tasting the second one and also finding it to be sour, the owner said in irritation, "So much of the day has passed yet you still don't know how to tell the difference between a sweet and a sour pomegranate. You need to *taste* it first."

Hadrat Ibrahim ibn Ad'ham ؇ replied, "But I've been entrusted to this garden to look after it, not to taste its fruits."

Hearing this, the man said, "Subhanallah! What a cautious and pious individual! Anyone would know that you are Ibrahim ibn Ad'ham ؇!"

Hadrat Ibrahim ibn Ad'ham ؇ then exited the garden and left behind its owner (who was still in amazement about whom he'd just met). – *Tazkiratul-Auliya, Pg. 124*

Lesson The Friends of Allah ؇ are trustworthy and do not cheat anyone in their promises. For this reason, those who have a negligent attitude towards the belongings of others should know that they are directly going against the teachings of Islam.

65 – THE DATE OF ANOTHER

Hadrat Ibrahim ibn Ad'ham ؇ was once resting alone in Baitul-Muqaddas. In the middle of the night, the door opened and an old man with a bright face came inside, followed by 40 people behind him. They all proceeded to the mihraab, read nafl Salaah and then backed up to sit down. One of them said, "Today there's someone in the musjid who's not from amongst us."

The old man smiled and replied, "Yes. He's Ibrahim ibn Ad'ham ؇. He hasn't received any pleasure from his worship for the last 40 days."

When Hadrat Ibrahim ibn Ad'ham ؇ heard this, he woke up, proceeded to the man and said, "What you said is true, but give me the reason why."

The old man replied, "You bought dates recently, but before you could take them home, someone else's date fell into your batch. Thinking that *all* belonged to you, you then picked them up and carried them away. By this date mixing into your wealth, it's now taking away the pleasure of your worship."

Hearing this, Hadrat Ibrahim ibn Ad'ham 🌼 went out into the city of Basra looking for the owner of this date until he finally found him and sought his forgiveness. – *Tazkiratul-Auliya, Pg. 125*

Lesson The Friends of Allah 🌼 are extremely cautious in their behaviour and are troubled by both doubtful and even *unintentional* things. Should one of them ever fall into such a predicament, however, Allah 🌺 assists them in removing this blemish and helps wipe away any fault in their actions. How oppressive then, are those who attribute lies and faults to the actions of the Saints?

We also come to know that not refraining oneself from Haraam and usurped wealth removes the pleasure of worship.

66 – THE POMEGRANATE OF THE WORSHIPPERS

Hadrat Muhammad Mubaarak 🌼 and Hadrat Ibrahim ibn Ad'ham 🌼 were once walking towards Baitul-Muqaddas when they saw a pomegranate tree along the way. Since it was midday, they decided to sit and rest under its shade for a while.

As they sat there, a voice was heard from the tree saying, "O Ibrahim 🌼, show me some favour and eat one of my pomegranates."

After the request was made a further two times, the two Saints broke a pomegranate off the tree and ate it (before walking away).

When they returned a year later, they found the same tree lush and dense. Not only were the pomegranates now much sweeter, the tree had even given its fruit twice in a single year! Due to these blessings, the people of the area gave it the name "رمان العابدين (The Pomegranate of the Worshippers)". – *Tazkiratul-Auliya, Pg. 126*

Lesson The Friends of Allah 🌺 bring blessings with them wherever they go and better the fate and prominence of whatever they touch. It's for this reason that one is hoped to become a better person and will better his actions by placing his hands in the hand of a Shaikh.

67 – A MESSAGE FROM ALLAH 🌺

Hadrat Bishr Haafi 🌼 was an alcoholic in the early stages of his life. Under the influence, he was once walking about when he saw a piece of paper lying on the ground with بسم الله الرحمن الرحيم written on it. In respect of the name of Allah ﷻ, he picked it up, bought some perfume to scent it with and placed it on a high place.

That night, a Saint who lived nearby was told in a dream, "Go and tell Bishr ؓ that because he scented Our name, showed respect to it and placed it on a high place, We will purify him, grant him sainthood in both this world and in the Hereafter and lift him up in status."

The Saint thought, "But Bishr is an alcoholic! Maybe there was a mistake in my dream."

He then woke up, made wudhu, read nafl Salaah and fell asleep again, only to be told the same thing once more. This occurred three more times with the following words included afterwards, "This message is truly for Bishr, so go and deliver it to him."

So, the Saint (knowing that Bishr Haafi was an alcoholic) went to the tavern the next day, stood outside it and called out for him. The people said that the person he was looking for was intoxicated and therefore out of his senses. Nevertheless, he replied, "Tell him in whichever way you can that there's a message for him and that the messenger is standing outside."

As requested, the people went to Bishr and said, "Wake up and go outside. There's someone with a message for you."

He replied, "Ask him who sent the message."

The Saint answered, "Tell him I've come with a message from Allah ﷻ. Who knows whether it's about rebuke or punishment?"

Bishr finally decided to go outside. After hearing the message, he sincerely repented from his actions and, from then on, reached such a high status as a Friend of Allah ﷻ that (due to the intensity of the observance of his Lord) he remained barefoot for the rest of his life and chose never to wear any shoes. This is why the word *haafi* ("barefoot") remains a title of his.

Whenever anyone asked him why he was barefoot, he'd reply, "Allah ﷻ states that He has spread the earth out for us, and whoever walks wearing shoes on a spread-out king's carpet is being disrespectful to the king." – *Tazkiratul-Auliya, Pg. 129*

Lesson If, from respecting such a small piece of paper, a sinner was elevated to the status of a Saint, how can we sinners not gain any benefit by respecting those who have the name of Allah ﷻ etched onto their hearts and are constantly engaged in His remembrance?

Also, if showing respect to the name of Allah ﷻ is beneficial to oneself, can showing respect to the name of the Beloved Prophet of Allah ﷺ by kissing one's thumbs, etc. upon hearing it [as was the action of Hadrat Abu

Bakr Siddique [2]] not bring any benefit? When Hadrat Bishr Haafi ◈ saw the name of Allah ◈, he scented it and was purified for this. So, when we engross ourselves in the remembrance of the Holy Prophet ◈ in any gathering and scent ourselves with perfume or rose-water, etc, will we not gain any benefit and pleasure from Allah ◈ in doing so?

We also learn that doing something that hasn't been prohibited by Islamic Law isn't a bad innovation. Otherwise, even the abandoning of shoes by Hadrat Bishr Haafi ◈ could be labelled so.

68 – RESPECT SHOWN BY ANIMALS

Hadrat Bishr Haafi ◈ remained barefoot for as long as he lived, and while he resided in Baghdad, no animal ever excreted on the streets in respect of the great Saint.

One day, an animal *did* leave its dung on the street, and when its owner saw this, he became concerned and thought that today may be the day Hadrat Bishr Haafi ◈ passed on.

A short while later, he was told that the demise of the great Saint had indeed come to pass. – *Tazkiratul-Auliya, Pg. 137*

Lesson When even animals show respect to the Friends of Allah ◈, why can't those who insult the Saints and attempt to sling mud onto their pure character be regarded as '*Like animals. In fact, even less.*' (Surah A'raaf (7), Verse 179)

69 – ZUN-NOON

Hadrat Zun-Noon Misri ◈ was once travelling somewhere on a ship, unknown to the passengers who he was. There was a merchant onboard who lost a pearl and began to accuse him of taking it. When he replied that he didn't, the merchant insisted that it was him and continued his abuse. Hadrat Zun-Noon Misri ◈ then turned his face towards the sky and said, "O Allah ◈! You know that I'm innocent of this accusation."

At once, thousands of fish, each with a pearl in its mouth, emerged from the sea, after which Hadrat Zun-Noon Misri ◈ took a pearl from one of them and gave it to the merchant!

Witnessing this miracle, the passengers onboard then fell to the feet of the great Saint and sought his forgiveness.

Noon ('fish') is the reason why he became famously known as *Zun-Noon* (The Person of the Fish). – *Tazkiratul-Auliya, Pg. 144*

Lesson When someone gives himself to Allah 🕮, Allah 🕮 gives everything of His to him, and His Friends 🕮 are so respected in creation that even fish serve and show their respect towards them. How unfortunate then are those who look down upon the Saints?!

70 – THE JEWELLER

Hadrat Zun-Noon Misri 🕮 once met a man who didn't believe in the Friends of Allah 🕮. So, he said to him, "Take this ring to a baker, ask him how much he'd pay for it, and then return."

When the man reached the bakery, the baker looked at the ring and said, "I wouldn't pay anything more than a dirham for this."

He then returned to Hadrat Zun-Noon Misri 🕮 and, after telling him how much the baker was willing to pay, was told, "Now go to a jeweller and ask him the same thing."

When the man reached the jeweller and showed him the very same ring, the jeweller said, "I'm prepared to give 1,000 dirhams for it."

The man returned once more to Hadrat Zun-Noon Misri 🕮 and gave him the news. The great Saint then said, "I consider your attitude towards the Friends of Allah 🕮 like that of the baker towards the ring. If you truly knew the status of the Saints, you'd never deny them."

Immediately, the man realized his mistake and decided to repent from his ways. – *Tazkiratul-Auliya, Pg. 145*

Lesson The denial of the Friends of Allah 🕮 is truly a reflection of one's own shortcomings. Indeed, only the people that have seen many Saints emanate from amongst them testify to their existence and serve and become disciples of them.

71 – THE VIOLIN

Hadrat Bā-Yazeed Bustaami 🕮 once saw a little boy playing a violin and said, "Laa Hawla wa Laa Quwwata Illa Billah."

This angered the boy, so he took the violin and struck Hadrat Bā-Yazeed Bustami 🕮 on the head with it, breaking it in the process and injuring the head of the great Saint.

Saying nothing, Hadrat Bā-Yazeed Bustaami ﷺ then proceeded to his home, gathered some sweetmeats and money to the value of the violin and had it sent to the boy with the following message, "You broke your violin on my head. Here's the money needed to buy another one, and the sweetmeats are for the trouble you've experienced in all of this."

When the boy heard this, he ran towards Hadrat Bā-Yazeed Bustaami ﷺ, fell to his feet and repented for his actions with great sorrow. (Even other boys repented from their ways upon seeing this.) – *Tazkiratul-Auliya, Pg. 175*

Lesson So eminent are the Friends of Allah ﷻ in character that they don't believe in one bad turn deserving another – a true reflection of the character of the Holy Prophet ﷺ,

> *"Salaam upon him who was good to his enemies.*
> *Salaam upon him who made dua for those who swore him."*

The key to the greatness of the Saints is truly in their following of Allah's ﷻ Beloved ﷺ. May Allah ﷻ also increase the love of him within us.

72 – MAN & DOG

Hadrat Bā-Yazeed Bustaami ﷺ was once walking with some disciples of his when they came to a very narrow pathway. As they entered it, he saw a dog walking towards him from the other side and decided to turn around and free the pathway for it.

Seeing this, one of his disciples thought, "Allah ﷻ has granted mankind such great stature and respect within His creation, yet Hadrat gives preference to this dog by turning around and letting it go through first."

Hadrat Bā-Yazeed Bustaami ﷺ was aware of his disciple's doubt and said, "I heard the dog say to me, 'O Bā-Yazeed ﷺ, it's only the glory of Allah ﷻ that He made me a dog from the very first day and clothed you with the title of *Sultaanul-Aarifeen* in the garb of humanity. At least take me as a creation of Allah ﷻ.'"

The Saint continued, "I was so overcome by these words that I decided to move out of its way in thanks to Allah ﷻ for what He had granted me." – *Tazkiratul-Auliya, Pg. 176*

Lesson It's truly the favour of Allah ﷻ that we were created, not as any despised creation, but as the best,

ولقد كرمنا بني آدم

'We have indeed honoured the sons of Adam ﷺ.'
– Surah Isra (17), Verse 70

This is why we are required to show humility and appreciation towards this favour (not pride and arrogance) and have mercy upon the rest of creation.

We also come to know that the Friends of Allah ﷻ are aware of the thoughts of their followers, just as how the Prophet ﷺ showed that he was aware of the thoughts of his Ummah.

73 – BĀ-YAZEED BUSTAAMI ﷺ & THE DOG

Hadrat Bā-Yazeed Bustaami ﷺ was once walking somewhere when he noticed a dog coming towards him. As they passed each other, he decided to lift up his garment to prevent it from coming into contact with it. The dog noticed this, stopped in its tracks and asked, "Sir, why did you just do that?"

He replied, "Because you're *najis* (impure)."

The dog then said, "If I *had* made your clothes impure, you could've just cleaned it with water, but if you did that out of pride and arrogance, thinking that you are greater than me, then even the seven seas couldn't clean the filth in your heart."

Hadrat Bā-Yazeed ﷺ replied, "You speak the truth, but you are *external* filth while pride and arrogance are both *internal*. O dog! I've learned a lot from you. Come be with us."

The dog replied, "We cannot be together because I'm a cursed creation who people throw stones at. You, on the other hand, are greeted as *Sultaanul-Aarifeen*. I collect bones for no purpose while human beings collect grain and store it in their homes."

Hadrat Bā-Yazeed Bustaami ﷺ then said, "Dog! Your words are truly insightful." – *Tazkiratul-Auliya, Pg. 172*

Lesson Mankind should do away with pride and arrogance as they are both filth of the heart and whose possessors are not worthy of the mercy of Allah ﷻ.

We also learn that the Friends of Allah ﷻ converse with animals (one of the many miracles granted to them), and that if man wishes, he can learn from something as disregarded as even a dog.

Hadrat Bā-Yazeed Bustaami ﷺ used to live next to a family of fire-worshippers. They had an infant son who'd cry whenever it got dark, and the father was so poor he couldn't afford to keep a candle lit for him.

One night, when the baby cried louder than usual, Hadrat Bā-Yazeed Bustaami ﷺ heard him, lit a candle, and left his house to stand outside theirs. By doing so, he was successful in soothing the baby and making the crying stop. This was done by him on the second and even the third night.

Seeing the character of the great Saint, the husband then said to his wife, "When the brightness of this Shaikh comes into our home, why should we still dawdle in the darkness of *kufr* (infidelity)? Come. Let's go serve the Shaikh and become Muslims."

So, they both approached Hadrat Bā-Yazeed Bustaami ﷺ, read the Kalima of Islam and lived the rest of their lives as believers. – *Tazkiratul-Auliya, Pg. 181*

Lesson *"Islam didn't spread through any book or college. It exists today due to the assistance of the pious."*

75 – THE REPLY TO MUNKAR & NAKEER

After the demise of Hadrat Bā-Yazeed Bustaami ﷺ, one of his disciples saw him in a dream and asked, "Hadrat, what answer did you give Munkar & Nakeer (the two angels of the grave)?"

He replied, "When they asked me the question, 'Who is your Lord?', I replied, "If I say I'm the servant of Allah ﷻ while He hasn't made me so, what difference would it make what I say? Go! First ask Allah ﷻ if I truly am His servant. If He agrees, *then* only am I successful." – *Tazkiratul-Auliya, Pg. 217*

Lesson Even though we regard ourselves Muslims, our true state is known only by Allah ﷻ and those He wishes to bestow this knowledge upon. So, whoever shows disrespect towards Islam after having entered it is as good as an ignorant person being called learned.

76 – A RICH & A POOR MAN

Hadrat Abdullah ibn Mubaarak ﷺ was a very wealthy individual of his time. He once took a poor person with him on Hajj and asked him during their journey, "We as wealthy individuals go for Hajj because we are asked to by Allah ﷻ. Why do you go?"

The man replied, "When a host is honourable, he welcomes the friend of his guest more than the guest himself. If you were called to Makkah, then so was I."

Hadrat Abdullah ibn Mubaarak ؓ then asked, "But what about Zakaat? Allah ﷻ only deals with the rich in that matter."

The man replied, "Yes, but who does He take it for? Of course, He only takes it to give it to the poor!"

This greatly affected Hadrat Abdullah ibn Mubaarak ؓ, and he then apologised to the man. – *Tazkiratul-Auliya, Pg. 220*

Lesson Don't look at the external appearance of the poor and needy. What they don't have in worldly material, they may have in piety and the love of Allah ﷻ – and that (more than money) is truly the benefactor of a person.

77 – POPULARITY

Hadrat Sufyaan Thauri ؓ once went out to read the Janaazah Salaah of a person and then returned home. After some time, he was told, "That person you read Janaazah for was so popular. No one ever spoke badly of him."

Hadrat Sufyaan Thauri ؓ replied, "If I'd known this, I wouldn't have read his Janaazah, because it means he never spoke the truth. Part of being truthful is that many people will hate you for it, but because everyone was happy with him, it means he agreed to whatever people said." – *Tazkiratul-Auliya, Pg. 233*

Lesson As many supporters the Friends of Allah ﷻ may have, so too do they have that many enemies. This is because the Saints don't hide their words when it comes to the truth, and for those who find the truth bitter, they can do nothing but hate them.

78 – ADVICE TO HAROON RASHID*

Hadrat Shafeeq Balkhi ؓ once reached the city of Baghdad during a Hajj trip and was summoned by the Khalifah of his time, Haroon Rashid. The Khalifah said to him, "You are the devout worshipper Shafeeq ؓ."

He replied, "I'm Shafeeq, yes, but not any devout worshipper."

The Khalifah requested, "Give me some advice."

Hadrat Shafeeq ﷺ replied, "Be attentive. Allah ﷻ gave you the position of Hadrat Abu Bakr Siddique ﷺ and requires that you be truthful like him. He gave you the position of Hadrat Umar ﷺ and requires that you distinguish between truth and falsehood like him. He gave you the position of Hadrat Uthman ﷺ and requires that you show humility and be kind to others like him, and He gave you the position of Hadrat Ali ﷺ and requires that you educate yourself and be just to the people like him."

Haroon Rashid replied, "May Allah ﷻ reward you. Tell me more."

Hadrat Shafeeq Balkhi ﷺ then said, "Allah ﷻ has a place called *Dozakh* (i.e. Jahannam) which He has consigned you as the doorkeeper of. He gave you three things to help keep people away from it – money, a whip and a sword. Whoever comes to you needy, give him money so that he doesn't turn away from Islam. Whoever goes against a command of Allah ﷻ, use the whip on him as a warning, and whoever kills someone, seek the justice of it through the sword. If you don't do these things, you'll be asked why on the Day of Judgement. A king is a river while his people are its streams. If you attain purity, they too will run pure."

The Khalifah replied, "May Allah ﷻ reward you! Tell me more."

Hadrat Shafeeq Balkhi ﷺ then said, "If you were in a jungle so thirsty that you were on the brink of death and finally came across a cup of water, how much would you pay for it?"

Haroon Rashid replied, "I'd give half my kingdom."

Hadrat Shafeeq Balkhi ﷺ continued, "And what if you couldn't pass urine after drinking it, again to the extent that you were on the brink of death, and someone suddenly came up to you and told you that he can help you pass it on condition that you give him the remainder of your kingdom? What would you do?"

The Khalifa answered, "I'll give it."

Hadrat Shafeeq Balkhi ﷺ then said, "So understand something – your kingdom is worth nothing more than a few sips of water and a few drops of urine. So, O king! Why show pride for something so contemptible?"

Hearing this, Haroon Rashid began to cry and said, "You speak the truth."

He then got up and sought leave from the Saint. – *Tazkiratul-Auliya, Pg. 243*

Lesson The Islamic Rulers of old believed in the Friends of Allah ﷻ, sought advice from them and even tried practicing upon their advice.

We also come to know that the Khalifah of his time is in reality the successor to the four initial Khalifahs (and the fulfilment of the rights of both Allah ﷻ *and* His creation is carried out by them).

Finally, the material things of this world (no matter how great) are of no value in the eyes of the pious.

79 – A KING IN A DERELICT HOUSE

The Khalifah of his time, Hadrat Haroon Rashid, once said to his minister, "My work has left me exhausted. Take me to the home of a pious individual so that I may rest for a while."

So, the minister suggested that they both go to Sufyaan Ainia.

When they reached his house, the minister knocked on the door and was asked by the one inside, "Who's there?"

He answered, "I've come with the Leader of the Muslims."

Sufyaan Ainia replied, "Why didn't you tell me he was coming so that I could've prepared myself?"

Hearing this, Haroon Rashid said to his minister, "This isn't the sort of person I was looking for."

The minister replied, "Then the complete individual you wish to meet can only be Fuzail Ayaaz ﷺ."

The Khalifah then said, "Then let's meet with him."

So, the two set off again, this time to the house of Hadrat Fuzail Ayaaz ﷺ, and when they reached it, they heard him inside reciting the following verse of the Holy Quran,

أم حسب الذين اجترحوا السيئات أن نجعلهم كالذين آمنوا

"Do those who seek after evil ways think that We will hold them equal with those who believe and do righteous deeds?"
– Surah Jathiya (45), Verse 21

Hearing this, Haroon Rashid jokingly remarked, "I came for advice and I've already received some."

The minister then knocked on the door, and Hadrat Fuzail Ayaaz ﷺ asked from within, "Who's there?"

He replied, "I've come with the Leader of the Muslims."

"What does he have to do with me? And what do I have to do with him? Don't disturb me."

The minister replied, "Obedience to the Khalifah is compulsory!"

"Stop troubling me."

"Give us permission to enter otherwise we'll come in by force!"

"I give you no such permission, but if you're going to come in by force, you're free to do as you wish."

These words had a tremendous effect on the Khalifah, and (together with the minister), he entered the house.

As they came inside, Hadrat Fuzail Ayaaz ﷺ put out his candle so that he wouldn't be able to see the face of Haroon Rashid. A moment later, their hands touched and he remarked, "How soft is this hand? It would be nice if it's saved from the fire of Hell."

He then began to read Salaah while the Khalifah broke out into tears.

After turning his head in Salaam, Hadrat Fuzail Ayaaz ﷺ was requested by the Khalifah to impart some advice to him, so he said, "Your ancestor, the uncle of the Holy Prophet ﷺ, once appealed to him, 'Make me the ruler of something.' The Prophet ﷺ replied, "O Uncle! I've made you the ruler of your *nafs*."

Haroon Rashid requested, "Tell me more."

The Saint continued, "When Hadrat Umar ibn Abdul-Aziz ﷺ was given the Caliphate, he said to the people, "I'm in the middle of a test and I seek advice on how to emerge successful from it."

They replied, "If you wish to be safe from the Fire, treat elderly Muslims as you'd treat your father, treat the youth as you'd treat your brother, treat children as you'd treat your children, and treat women as you'd treat your mother and sister – all with good behaviour."

Haroon Rashid persisted, "Tell me more."

Hadrat Fuzail Ayaaz ﷺ continued, "Be affectionate towards the pious, be good to your brothers, and do good to children. O Haroon Rashid! I hope that the Fire of Jahannam doesn't touch your handsome face. It was once said, 'كم من امير هناك اسير' How many leaders here will be prisoners in the Hereafter?!'"

Haroon Rashid began to cry again, this time even more so. Still, he asked for more advice and was told, "Prepare your answers for the questions of Allah ﷻ. He will question every Muslim concerning your leadership and will seek justice for all. If even one woman went to sleep hungry on any night, she will grab you by your clothes on the Day of Judgment and contend with you about it!"

Hearing this, the Khalifah burst into tears and cried so much this time that he lost consciousness. The minister pleaded, "Stop! You've killed him!"

Hadrat Fuzail Ayaaz ﷺ replied, "Be quiet. I'm killing the flattery from you!"

When the Khalifah awoke, he asked Hadrat Fuzail ﷺ, "Do you owe anyone anything?"

The Saint replied, "Yes, I owe a debt to Allah ﷻ, which is His obedience. If He seizes me without me having paid it, it would be truly unfortunate."

Haroon Rashid replied, "I mean any debt to people."

Hadrat Fuzail Ayaaz ﷺ answered, "Alhamdulillah, Allah ﷻ has granted me tremendous favours and I have no complaint against them."

The Khalifah then gave him a bag of 1,000 dinars, saying, "This money is Halaal. I acquired it from the inheritance of my mother."

The Saint became angry upon hearing this and said, "All the advice I've given has now become useless! I call you towards success and the severing of worldly ties and you want to throw me into destruction!? Whatever you have, give it to those who deserve it. You, however, prefer giving it to those you shouldn't."

He then got up and left them for another room, closing the door behind him.

The Khalifah then too got up and exited the house with his minister. As they headed back, he turned to his minister and said, "He really is a man of truth and a friend of Allah ﷻ." – *Tazkiratul-Auliya, Pg. 94-6*

Lesson Whoever gains the recognition of Allah ﷻ loses interest in anything besides Him. They are our true, spiritual leaders, and in the past, even political leaders would seek their advice at their doorstep.

نعم الامير على باب الفقير
"How great are the wealthy at the door of a beggar!"

We also learn that the greater a person's responsibility is in this world, the more accountable he will be on the Last Day.

The ruler of Nishapur, Abdullah ibn Taahir, once returned after a leave of absence and was welcomed by the city upon his arrival. For three days, everyone big and small came out to see him, and when there was no one left for him to greet, he asked, "Is there anyone else who hasn't come to meet me?"

The people replied, "Just two people, Hadrat Ahmed Harb ؑ and Hadrat Aslam Too'si ؑ."

Abdullah ibn Taahir asked, "Why didn't they come?"

They answered, "They are both Islamic scholars and friends of Allah ﷻ. They don't come out to meet kings."

The king respectfully replied, "Well, if they didn't come out to see me, we'll go and see them."

He then set off to the house belonging to the first (Hadrat Ahmed Harb ؑ).

When Hadrat Ahmed Harb ؑ was told that the king was on his way, he replied, "In that case, we will have to meet."

Upon the king's arrival, the great Saint lowered his head in order not see him. He then lifted it up after some time and said, "I was told that you were handsome, and indeed today I see it for myself. O Abdullah! Don't let that be a means to destroy you in going against the commands of Allah ﷻ."

Hearing this, Abdullah ibn Taahir sought leave from Hadrat Ahmed Harb ؑ and proceeded to the house of Hadrat Aslam Too'si ؑ.

Upon his arrival, the door of the great Saint's house was shut and he refused to grant him permission to enter. However, knowing that he would ultimately have to come out for Salaah, Abdullah ibn Taahir decided to remain waiting outside for him.

As expected, Hadrat Aslam Too'si ؑ eventually did emerge from his house at the time of Salaah, and as soon as Abdullah ibn Taahir laid eyes on him, he descended from his horse, kissed the feet of the great Saint and said, "O Allah ﷻ! Your friend shows enmity towards me, which is why I'm a terrible person! I love him, which is why he is beloved! By means of this good, make me good too!"

The Saint then made dua personally for the king before kindly seeking leave from him. – *Tazkiratul-Auliya, Pg. 290*

Lesson The Saints are our spiritual rulers, and this rank was gained by them due their obedience to the laws of only Allah ﷻ and His Beloved Messenger ﷺ.

We also learn that through the mediation of something good, Allah ﷻ can show favour even to something bad.

81 – BAHRAAM THE FIRE-WORSHIPPER

Hadrat Ahmed Harb ◌ used to live next to a fire-worshipper. After once hearing that he'd been robbed of some money, he said to some of his friends, "Let's meet our neighbour Bahraam. He's been heartbroken since that incident."

So, after going to his house and knocking on the door, Bahraam opened it and was pleased to see that one of the leading Imams of the community had come to visit him. He kissed the cuff of Hadrat Ahmed Harb ◌ and respectfully seated them all.

Hadrat Ahmed ◌ then asked him, "Friend, we learnt that your money was stolen, so we came to see how you're doing."

Bahraam replied, "Yes, it did happen, but I'm still grateful for three things. One, that it was my wealth that was stolen, not the wealth of another. Two, that they stole only half of my money and I'm still left with the other half, and three, that they only stole something of worldly value while I still have my faith."

Hearing these intellectual words, Hadrat Ahmed Harb ◌ said to his friends, "Take note that the fragrance of friendship emanates from Bahraam."

He then turned to Bahraam and said, "Why do you worship fire?"

Bahraam replied, "So that on the Day of Judgment, it will not harm me. The more wood I feed it in this life, the more faithful it will be to me after death and help me get closer to Allah ﷻ."

Hadrat Ahmed Harb ◌ respectfully said, "You're mistaken. Fire is a very weak thing. If a little boy throws just a handful of water over it, it's extinguished. Ask yourself then, how could such a weak thing become so great on its own?

"Another thing is, fire is ignorant: it doesn't care whether there's dirt or musk in front of it, both will burn without discrimination. It wouldn't even save you even though you worship it."

These words began to affect the heart of Bahraam. So, he said, "Answer these questions, and if your answers are good, I'll become a Muslim."

Hadrat Ahmed Harb ◌ replied, "Ask what you wish."

Bahraam began, "Why did the Creator create? After creating, why does He sustain? After sustaining, why does He take away life? And after taking away life, why does He give it back?"

Hadrat Ahmed Harb ﷺ answered, "He created us so that we may know Him as the Creator. He sustains us so that we may know Him as the Sustainer. He takes away life so that we may know Him as still in control over us, and He brings us back so that we may know His power."

Bahraam then said, "Place your hand in this fire. If it doesn't burn you, I'll accept Islam."

So, after saying 'Bismillah', Hadrat Ahmed Harb ﷺ placed his hand in the fire (and kept it there for some time). When Bahraam saw that it had no effect on him, he then read the Kalima of Islam and became a Muslim! – *Tazkiratul-Auliya, Pg. 295*

Lesson Whether they are believers or not, the Friends of Allah ﷻ are always concerned about the wellbeing of their neighbours.

We also learn that anyone can benefit from showing respect to the Saints (even if he is a non-Muslim).

82 – THE SHROUD THIEF

Hadrat Haatim Asum ﷺ was once delivering a lecture in the city of Balkh. During his speech, he proclaimed, "O Allah ﷻ! Grant Your mercy to the biggest sinner in this gathering."

There was a shroud thief present within this crowd. When night fell, he left for the graveyard (as usual) and began to dig up one of the graves. Before he could jump inside, he heard a voice from the unseen saying, "O thief! You were granted mercy today in the gathering of Haatim Asum ﷺ, so why do you return to commit the same sin again?!"

Hearing this, the thief began to cry and then sincerely repented from his ways. – *Tazkiratul-Auliya, Pg. 297*

Lesson Sinners can be forgiven by Allah ﷻ simply by being present in the company of His Friends ﷺ.

83 – SHAITAAN'S DESPAIR

Hadrat Haatim Asum ﷺ once said, "Shaitaan once tried to trick me with a few questions, but I gave him answers that made him despondent and helped me get rid of him. He asked me, "What will you eat?"

I replied, "Death."
"What will you wear?"
"My shroud (kafan)."
"Where will you stay?"
"In my grave."
Hearing these words, he then said to me, "You're a tough individual." –
Tazkiratul-Auliya, Pg. 301

Lesson Shaitaan has no hold over those Allah ﷻ wishes to protect.

84 – THE SAINT'S WIFE

Hadrat Haatim Asum ؓ was once planning a long trip away from home and told his wife, "I'm going to be away for four months. How would you like me to provide expenditure for you while I'm gone?"
She answered, "The way you provide me with my life."
The Saint then said, "But your life isn't in my hands!"
His wife replied, "So why should my sustenance be too?"

Some time later, after Hadrat Haatim Asum ؓ had left, an old woman asked his wife, "How much did he leave for you?"
She answered, "The one who requires sustenance has left, but the One Who provides it is still with me." – *Tazkiratul-Auliya, Pg. 301*

Lesson Throughout Islamic history, the Ummah of Sayyiduna Rasoolullah ﷺ has also seen many women emerge who were prominently pious and who ultimately depended upon no-one but Allah ﷻ.

85 – TRAVEL PREPARATIONS

A man once met Hadrat Haatim ؓ during a journey and said to him, "Hadrat, give me some advice."
The Saint replied, "If you want a friend in life, Allah ﷻ is sufficient. If you want fellow-travellers, the angels on your shoulders [who record your deeds] are sufficient. If you want a warning, the world is sufficient. If you want a consoler and comforter, the Quran is sufficient. If you need something to do, worship is sufficient. If you need someone to lecture to you, death is sufficient, and if you don't like these words of mine, Jahannam (Hell) will be sufficient." – *Tazkiratul-Auliya, Pg. 302*

Lesson The worship and remembrance of Allah ﷻ are all one needs for his or her destination while on this journey through life.

86 – MAN'S WEALTH

Someone once said to Hadrat Haatim Asum ◈, "A certain person has accumulated great wealth."
He replied, "Will he live longer through it?"
The man said, "No."
Hadrat then asked, "So what's the wealth of man good for?" – *Tazkiratul-Auliya, Pg. 304*

87 – THE SALAAH OF A SAINT

Someone once asked Hadrat Haatim Asum ◈, "Hadrat, how do you read Salaah?"
The great Friend of Allah ◈ replied, "When the time for Salaah arrives, I make both a physical and spiritual wudhu, the first with water and the second with *tauba* (repentance). I then enter the musjid and observe the Kaaba with the Maqaam-e-Ibrahim between my two eyebrows. I place *Jannah* (Heaven) on my right, Jahannam on my left and the *Siraat* (bridge) under my feet. I think of the Angel of Death ◈ behind me and turn my heart towards Allah ﷻ. (In fact, I entrust it to Him.) I then say 'Allahu-Akbar' with great respect, stand in honour, recite the Holy Quran in awe and go into ruku & sajda with humility. Finally, I sit in tranquility and make Salaam in thankfulness. That's how I read Salaah." – *Tazkiratul-Auliya*

Lesson The Friends of Allah ﷻ have shown us the correct and complete way to read Salaah. How then can we, who are guilty of so many mistakes in our Salaah, not take heed and be more attentive in it?!

88 – THE KNOWLEDGE OF THE SAINTS

Hadrat Sahl ibn Abdullah Tastari ◈ once said to his friends, "I remember well when Allah ﷻ asked everyone (on the Day of Covenant when all souls were in front of Him), "الست بربكم Am I not your Lord?" and I replied, "Of course!"

I also remember being in the womb of my mother, and even reading Salaah every night with my uncle Muhammad ibn Sawaar ۩ when I was just three years old." – *Tazkiratul-Auliya*

Lesson The Friends of Allah ۩ have knowledge of and have been aware of their existence from the very first day their souls were created. How then can the Beloved Prophet of Allah ﷺ, who is the teacher and leader of all of them, not have had this quality in him too?!

We also learn that the pious occupied themselves in the worship of Allah ۩ even when they were little. So, can those who haven't even begun to read Salaah in their old age ever hope to be pious themselves?

89 – THE DUA OF THE SAINTS

A governor by the name of Umar Waleeth once fell sick and couldn't be cured by any doctor. Someone eventually suggested, "Medication isn't helping. You should seek the assistance of someone whose supplications are constantly accepted by Allah ۩."

Hearing this, everyone agreed that such a person was Hadrat Sahl ۩, a pious and renowned individual of the time.

When the governor called for Hadrat Sahl ۩, he agreed to come as per the instruction of the verse "و اولى الامر منكم [Obey] those charged with authority amongst you." [4] He sat next to the governor and said, "Dua is accepted from any individual who turns to Allah ۩ and repents with a sincere heart. O Umar! There are people in your jail who've done nothing wrong. Release them first before repenting. After that, I'll make dua."

So, as instructed, Umar Waleeth released the prisoners and began to repent for his ways. Hadrat Sahl ۩ then lifted up his hands and said, "O Allah ۩, just as how You've shown him disgrace due to his disobedience, show him the respect I've earned by being in Your obedience. Just as how You've clothed his inner-self with repentance, clothe his outer-self with peace."

As Hadrat Sahl ۩ was making this supplication, the governor found that he had been completely cured! The great Saint was then offered some gifts by him (but he declined them). – *Tazkiratul-Auliya, Pg. 312*

Lesson Where dawā (medication) ends, dua begins, and duas have a better chance of being accepted when made close to the pious and with a sincere heart.

We also learn that the supplication of a Saint can change the fate of a person.

90 – A SURPRISING DUA

Hadrat Ma'roof Karkhi ﷺ was once walking along the edge of the Tigris River with some of his followers when they noticed a boat containing a number of young people involved in sinful play and amusement. They said, "Hadrat, why don't you make dua for these people to drown so that their evil doesn't spread to anywhere else?"

The Saint replied, "Raise your hands and make dua with me, but say 'Ameen' to whatever I say."

So, after everyone raised their hands as instructed, Hadrat Ma'roof Karkhi ﷺ implored, "O Allah ﷻ, just as how You have given them happiness and enjoyment in this world, give it to them in the Hereafter."

His followers were taken aback by this and asked him why such a supplication was made. Hadrat Ma'roof ﷺ replied, "Wait here. You'll see what I intended to do."

After a short while, the people on the boat laid eyes on Hadrat Ma'roof Karkhi ﷺ and immediately broke their musical instruments, threw away their alcohol and began to cry bitterly. They then reached the shore and fell at the feet of the great Saint, repenting from their ways.

Hadrat Ma'roof ﷺ then turned to his followers and said, "See? We got what we wanted without these people drowning or being put into any difficulty." – *Tazkiratul-Auliya, Pg. 330*

Lesson The duas of the Friends of Allah ﷻ can change the condition of people, and those things that can't be changed with a sword can be changed in an instant by just the glance of a Saint.

91 – THE ASHAMED GOVERNOR

The uncle of Hadrat Ma'roof Karkhi ﷺ was the governor of the city. He was once walking in a jungle when he saw his nephew sitting somewhere eating bread with a dog beside him. Hadrat Ma'roof ﷺ was breaking a piece off for himself, placing it in his mouth, and thereafter breaking a piece off for the dog and placing it in its mouth.

The governor asked him, "Don't you have any shame, eating with a dog?!"

Hadrat Ma'roof Karkhi ⚜ replied, "Actually, it's because I *have* shame that I'm feeding it."

The Saint then looked up to a bird that was flying above him and called out to it. In response, the bird immediately flew into his hand and covered its eyes and mouth with its wing.

Hadrat Ma'roof Karkhi ⚜ then looked at the governor and said, "Whoever has shame in front of Allah ﷻ, His creation will have shame in front of him."

Seeing this, the governor then aptly lowered his *own* head in shame! – *Tazkiratul-Auliya, Pg. 331*

Lesson The pious are possessors of excellent character and constantly assist the creation for the sake of Allah ﷻ (even if it means feeding a dog). How hard then is the heart that feels no sorrow for the human being that goes to sleep hungry every night?

We also come to know that serving the poor and needy is, in fact, a type of shame and modesty.

It is also clear that even animals serve the Friends of Allah ⚜.

92 – THE PLACE OF DEMISE

Hadrat Fath Mosuli ⚜ was once sitting in the musjid with some friends of his when a young boy with simple clothes walked in and asked him, "Sir! Does a traveler have any rights?"

He replied, "Yes, he does."

The boy then said, "I'm a traveler. I'm currently staying at a certain place and tomorrow will be the day I leave the world. I want you to find me there, give me ghusl and bury me in these clothes."

He then turned around and walked away.

The next day, Hadrat Fath Mosuli ⚜ proceeded to the place he was directed to and indeed found that the boy had left this world. As requested, he personally carried out his ghusl and wrapped the boy up in the clothes he was wearing.

As soon as he was done, the boy's hand emerged out of the kafn and grabbed the clothing of Hadrat Fath ⚜. The boy then said, "Jazakallah,

Fath Mosuli ⚬. If Allah ﷻ chooses to grant me any status, I will repay you for this service you have done for me." – *Tazkiratul-Auliya, Pg. 349*

Lesson In following the commands of Allah ﷻ, the pious servants reach such high ranks that they eventually come to know of the date of their demise.

We also learn that the Saints do not truly die. They simply leave one world for another – as one writer attests,

> *"Don't say that the Friends of Allah ﷻ are dead.*
> *They have simply left this world for their true abode."*

93 – LANTERNS

A pious man once came to the house of Hadrat Ahmed Khadrawiya ⚬. So, to brighten his home, Hadrat Ahmed ⚬ lit seven candles inside.

The man asked him, "Why did you trouble yourself?"

Hadrat Ahmed ⚬ replied, "Get up and put out every candle that wasn't lit in the path of Allah ﷻ."

The man then stood up and tried to put them out but soon realized that none of the flames could be extinguished!

The next day, both were walking together when they reached a nearby church and saw one of the priests sitting at the door. The priest looked at them and said, "The table-spread's out. Come and eat."

Hadrat Ahmed ⚬ replied, "Friends don't eat with enemies."

The priest then said, "Then make me a Muslim," and he thereafter read the Kalima of Islam, along with seventy of his followers who were sitting nearby!

That night, Hadrat Ahmed Khadrawiya ⚬ heard a voice in his sleep say, "You lit seven candles in Our path, so We lit seventy hearts with noor and Imaan through you." – *Tazkiratul-Auliya, Pg. 360*

Lesson Any work that is done for the pleasure of Allah ﷻ is not wastage. How then can spending money and time for the pleasure of the Beloved Prophet of Allah ﷺ in gatherings celebrating his birth and history, etc. be wastage and detestable?!

Hadrat Yahya Muaaz Raazi ﷺ had a brother who left his home to work as an attendant in the Haram of the Kaaba. He once sent a letter back to Hadrat Yahya ﷺ stating, "I desired three things in my life and attained two so far. First, I wished to reside in a good and blessed place, and today I work around the Kaaba, the most blessed of all places. Second, I wished to gain someone who could assist me and prepare my water for wudhu, and now I have such a person. My third wish is that I see you before I leave this world, and I hope that Allah ﷻ will assist me in this."

In response, Hadrat Yahya Muaaz Raazi ﷺ wrote, "You sought to work in a good place, now try to instill good within you. After that, you may reside wherever you wish. Remember: places don't give people respect. On the contrary, places are given respect by those who reside there.

"You also said that you sought a servant for you. If you were kind and generous, you wouldn't make a fellow slave of Allah ﷻ one of your slaves and deter him from the service of his Lord by busying him with your affairs. You should wish to be a servant yourself and not someone who is served by others. Remember that being served is a quality of Allah ﷻ, and a slave who wishes to be served is still a slave. When someone believes he possesses a quality of Allah ﷻ, he drowns himself in pride and arrogance.

"Lastly, you said that you wish to see me. Know that if you were truly engrossed in the remembrance of Allah ﷻ, you would have no time to think of anyone else but Him. Try to attain this level of His remembrance so that even the thought of your family doesn't come into you. Brother! *If you gain Allah ﷻ, what would you need from me? And if you don't gain Allah ﷻ, what benefit will I be to you?*" – *Tazkiratul-Auliya*, Pg. 368

Lesson The duty of man is to first perfect his actions. After that, he may live wherever he wishes.

One should also try to instill humility within oneself and avoid being served as much as possible (as this may instill arrogance within us).

95 – THE INTERPRETATION OF DREAMS

Hadrat Yahya Muaaz Raazi ﷺ once wrote to a friend, "The world is akin to a dream, and the Hereafter to being awake. When someone cries in a dream, its interpretation is the exact opposite in this world (i.e. he will laugh and be happy). So, friend, you should cry in this world in fear of

Allah ﷻ so that you may laugh when you awake [in the Hereafter]." –
Tazkiratul-Auliya, Pg. 369

Lesson Adorn your Hereafter with good deeds while in this life and live in
the fear of Allah ﷻ so that you may ultimately be included amongst the
successful.

96 – FOUR SUPPLICATIONS

There was a minister who always involved himself in sin and never
bothered to correct his ways. He had a slave whom he once gave four
dirhams to and ordered him to buy sweetmeats at a local bazaar.

As the slave walked towards the market, he came across a group of people
who were listening to a talk by Hadrat Mansoor ؏, so he stopped and
thought, "Let me listen to what Hadrat Mansoor ؏ is saying."

During the speech, Hadrat Mansoor ؏ wished to assist a dervish and
appealed to the crowd saying, "Whoever gives this dervish four dirhams, I
will make four supplications of his choice in return."

The servant thought, "Let me be the one to serve him."

So, he gave his four dirhams to the dervish and requested the following
four duas to be made by Hadrat Mansoor ؏: 1) That he be freed as a slave.
2) That he regain the four dirhams he just spent. 3) That his minister
realizes his errors and changes his ways, 4) and that himself, his minister
and all those present in that gathering be forgiven by Allah ﷻ.

After Hadrat Mansoor ؏ made these four duas, the slave then left the
gathering and returned back to the minister's residence.

When the minister saw him, he asked, "What took you so long?"

The servant then related the entire incident to him, after which the
minister said, "Well, your first three duas are all accepted. I've freed you
from being a slave and grant you 400 dirhams in replacement for those
four. I've also come to realize my mistakes and hope to never be
disobedient to Allah ﷻ again. As for the fourth dua, that's not in my
power to give."

At that moment, a sound was heard from the unseen saying, "O slave!
After submitting yourself to Us, you chose to do everything you could in
your power. Why then should We, the Most Merciful, not do everything
We are asked? Go, We have taken all of you into Our mercy and have
forgiven the two of you, along with all those who were present in the
gathering." – *Tazkiratul-Auliya, Pg. 415*

Lesson Gatherings held in the remembrance of Allah ﷻ are places upon which His mercy descends.

We also come to know that assisting the needy is certainly a way to gain His happiness.

Also, asking the pious to make dua for you is a stronger way to supplicate than making dua on your own, as Allah ﷻ states in a Hadith, "لئن سالنى لاعطينه" When my (accepted) servant asks of Me, I will surely grant it to him."

97 – THE INTUITION OF A TRUE BELIEVER

There was a fire-worshipper during the time of Hadrat Junaid Baghdadi ﷺ who once put on his *zunnar* (a cross-thread garment worn by non-Muslims) and covered it with the clothes of a Muslim. He then approached the great Saint and said, "Sir! I came to ask you about the Hadith,

اتقوا بفراسة المؤمن فانه ينظر بنور الله

"Beware the intuition of a true believer, for indeed he sees with the noor of Allah ﷻ."

"What does it mean?"

Hadrat Junaid Baghdadi ﷺ replied, "It means you must tear your inner garment and embrace Islam."

Hearing this, the fire-worshipper immediately read the Kalima and became a Muslim! – *Tazkiratul-Auliya, Pg. 433*

Lesson The Friends of Allah ﷺ are the possessors of true Imaan, and so nothing can be hidden from them.

Also, in accordance to the abovementioned Hadith, Imam Jalaaluddin Rumi ﷺ writes, "The Lauh-e-Mahfooz (sacred Tablet upon which everything is written) is constantly in front of the Friends of Allah ﷺ (i.e. they may read it whenever they wish)."

98 – BACKBITING

Hadrat Junaid Baghdadi ﷺ once saw a man begging and thought, "Why's that man begging when he's perfectly healthy and can earn a living instead?"

That night, he saw some people in a dream presenting a large tray to him with a lid over it, instructing him to eat what was inside.

After lifting the lid and seeing that it was the corpse of the man he'd seen earlier, Hadrat Junaid Baghdadi ؓ said, "I don't eat dead bodies."

They replied, "Then why did you do just that during the day?"

Hearing this, Hadrat Junaid ؓ realized what this was all about and woke up in a fright. He then made wudhu, read two rakaats Salaah, and thereafter went out to look for the man – eventually finding him on a riverbank gathering together and eating the herbs that people were washing away.

As he came towards to him, the man lifted his head and said, "O Junaid ؓ! It's my right that you make tauba for the thought you had of me."

Hadrat Junaid Baghdadi ؓ replied, "I know."

The man then said, "Now go. هو الذى يقبل التوبة عن عباده 'It's Allah ﷻ Who accepts the repentance of his bondsmen.' Safeguard your heart from now onwards." – *Tazkiratul-Auliya, Pg. 440*

Lesson Backbiting is a serious offence and is akin to eating the flesh of your dead brother.

We also see again that nothing is hidden from the Friends of Allah ؓ.

99 – THE BLACKNESS OF THE MOUTH

Hadrat Junaid Baghdadi ؓ had a disciple in Basra who once intended to commit a sin. As soon as this disciple spoke of it, a blackness appeared over his mouth and terrified him so much that he ran into his house and decided he wouldn't come out!

Within three days, the blackness lessened until it was finally gone, and the disciple found that his mouth was now bright.

On that day, someone arrived at his doorstep and handed him a letter from Hadrat Junaid Baghdadi ؓ. In it was written, "Control your heart and live respectfully as a worshipper from now on. I've had to perform the duties of a cleaner for the last three days to remove that blackness from your mouth." – *Tazkiratul-Auliya, Pg. 446*

Lesson Peers help to save their disciples from sin no matter how far they may be. So, one should sincerely become the disciple of a murshid so that one may better oneself in one's actions more easily.

We also learn that the body emanates light when one's thought is constantly on Allah ﷻ and becomes dark when one is engrossed in sin.

Hadrat Junaid Baghdadi 🌷 once came across a descendent of the Holy Prophet 🌷 and asked him, "Where are you from?"

The man replied, "Jilaan."

"Who are you a descendant of?"

He answered, "Hadrat Ali 🌷."

Hadrat Junaid Baghdadi 🌷 then said, "Your ancestor (i.e. Hadrat Ali 🌷) had two swords in his possession – one to use against disbelievers and one against his carnal desires. Tell me, which sword do you use?"

The man began to cry and said, "You should guide me and give me some advice, since you've already taught me so much." – *Tazkiratul-Auliya, Pg. 448*

Lesson Even if there are no physical wars to fight, a Muslim is constantly at war with himself and should always strive against his *nafs*.

101 – SHAITAAN'S TRAP

Hadrat Abdullah Jilaa 🌷 once saw a beautiful woman amongst the fire-worshippers and began to stare at her in awe of her beauty. When Hadrat Junaid Baghdadi 🌷 walked by him, Hadrat Abdullah 🌷 said, "O teacher, I've been reflecting over the beauty of this girl, thinking how it will burn in the fire of Jahannam."

Hadrat Junaid Baghdadi 🌷 replied, "Abdullah 🌷! It's the trickery of Shaitaan and deceit of the nafs which you are truly fascinated with. You are seeing that woman out of lust, not because she's a warning to you. If you truly wanted something to remind you of the punishment in the Hereafter, there are 18,000 realms full of wonder for you to observe, yet you take this trap of Shaitaan as a good thing. Soon you'll see the outcome of it."

Hadrat Abdullah 🌷 was also a hafiz. After this incident, he forgot the entire Quran and cried for years to Allah 🌷 in repentance until it finally came back to memory again. From then on, he paid no attention to anything he saw. – *Tazkiratul-Auliya, Pg. 497*

There was a villager in the time of Hadrat Abul-Hasan Bu'Shaikhi ؓ who lost one of his donkeys and immediately ran to the great Shaikh saying, "You're the one who took it!"

Hadrat Abul-Hasan ؓ replied, "Today's the first day I've ever seen you. What would I possibly need from your donkey? Go away and stop accusing me."

The villager continued, "I'm not going and I'll even shout it out! You stole my donkey!"

Hadrat Abul-Hasan ؓ then lifted his hands in dua and said, "O Allah ﷻ, give me a solution to this man's dilemma."

At that moment, a man arrived and told the villager that they had found his donkey elsewhere. The villager immediately fell to the feet of Hadrat Abul-Hasan Bu'Shaikhi ؓ and said, "O Hadrat ؓ, forgive me! I knew you didn't take it, but I also knew that you are favored in the court of Allah ﷻ, and I thought that if I trouble you, you'll make dua for me, and in this way I'll get my donkey back. I'm happy to see that that's exactly what happened." – *Tazkiratul-Auliya, Pg. 529*

Lesson Even non-Scholars know that duas made by the pious are more readily answered by Allah ﷻ and that presenting oneself in front of them helps one attain a solution to their problems sooner. Can those who now think of themselves as equal to the Saints be better than this villager?

103 – AFTER THE PROPHET'S ﷺ TIME*

The great Saint, Hadrat Hakeem Tirmidhi ؓ, was a very handsome individual. A wealthy woman once became infatuated with him and approached him to let him know of her feelings for him. He responded by saying 'Laa Hawla…' and thereafter walked away.

Thirty years later, as an elderly man, he recalled this incident and thought, "What harm would there have been if I chose not to break her heart and then make tauba afterwards?"

Hadrat Hakeem ؓ was immediately startled by this and began to reproach his nafs saying, "You didn't even think about that when you were young, how could you consider it now after having performed so much worship and *mujaahidah* (strife against one's desires)?!"

He then began crying tears of sadness and remained disillusioned for three days until he eventually saw the Holy Prophet ﷺ in a dream saying to him, "Tirmidhi ﷺ, don't be sad. This is no fault of yours, because more than thirty years have passed since my demise, and you're now far from that era. It's the effect of this distance that you think such things. Don't grieve, and continue making the zikr of Allah ﷻ." – *Tazkiratul-Auliya, Pg. 535*

Lesson The Friends of Allah ﷻ are troubled by their bad intentions even if they don't intend committing them. How then can we fearlessly commit sin every day and feel no remorse?

We also see that the Prophet ﷺ himself consoles the close servants of Allah ﷻ, and that the further we are from his era, the more trials and tribulations we will face in the world.

104 – THE TWO SŪFIS

Two Sūfis once traveled from afar to meet the renowned Hadrat Abdullah Haneef ﷺ. When they reached his school, they were told that he'd gone to the king's court. Hearing this, they asked themselves in surprise, "What kind of Saint presents himself in the king's court?!"

Nevertheless, they now had some time to spare, so they decided to walk in the city and eventually came across a nearby tailor. Knowing that their clothing was in bad shape, they entered his place, asked him for a needle and began to patch their garments.

While inside, the tailor noticed that his scissors were missing and accused the two of having taken it. When they denied this, he grabbed them both and took them to the king, saying, "These two stole a pair of scissors from me!"

At that time, Hadrat Abdullah Haneef ﷺ was also present in the king's court and said, "These two are Sūfi-inclined. They couldn't have done such a thing. Release them."

As requested, both were then freed. Hadrat Abdullah Haneef ﷺ then looked at the two men and said, "Your bad thought of me was unwarranted. This is the type of work I do in the king's court."

Seeing this miracle of his, the two then decided to become his disciples. – *Tazkiratul-Auliya, Pg. 571*

Lesson Those who undermine the Friends of Allah ﷻ very quickly land themselves in difficulty.

Hadrat Abu Muhammad Jareeri ﷺ once said, "For the last forty years, I've been looking for a white hawk but I haven't found one even until today."

His disciples replied, "Hadrat, please explain."

Hadrat Abu Muhammad ﷺ began, "Forty years ago, I completed my Asr Salaah in the musjid and noticed a young, frail man with bare feet and disheveled hair entering it with his head down. He made wudhu, read his Asr Salaah and sat down (with his head still lowered) until Maghrib Salaah. After reading Maghrib with jama'ah, he then continued to sit in the same manner again.

That day, the Khalifa invited all of the pious individuals to his residence for an evening meal. So, I went up to this man and said, "I'm going to the Khalifa's house on his invitation. Are you coming?"

He replied, "I don't care about the invitation, but if you wish, bring some sweetmeats back for me."

I paid no attention to this statement and made my way to the feast.

On my return, I found the man still in the musjid with his head lowered and said nothing to him. I then read Esha Salaah, headed back home and fell off to sleep.

That night, I saw Rasoolullah ﷺ in a dream surrounded by other prophets including Hadrat Ibrahim ﷺ and Hadrat Musa ﷺ. When I made Salaam to them, the Prophet ﷺ turned his face away from me, so I asked him, "O Rasoolullah ﷺ! Did I do something wrong?"

He replied, "One of our friends requested sweetmeats from you, but you ignored him."

Hearing this, I woke up alarmed and began to cry. I then immediately made my way to the musjid and saw the man leaving, so I shouted to him, "Sir, wait a while! I'll bring some sweetmeats for you."

He replied, "It now becomes easy for you when someone brings the intervention of Rasoolullah ﷺ and other prophets with him. You found it very difficult a short while ago."

He then turned and walked away. – *Tazkiratul-Auliya, Pg. 574*

Lesson Even according to the Hadith, there are many elevated servants in the kingdom of Allah ﷺ who present themselves as weak and untidy. These individuals should never be looked at with contempt.

It's also clear that the respect of the Friends of Allah ﷻ is also the respect of the Beloved Prophet ﷺ himself, and that insulting them is enough to earn the displeasure of Rasoolullah ﷺ (and therefore ultimately Allah ﷻ).

106 – THE WISE STUDENT

Hadrat Junaid ﷺ had many disciples but always focused on one in particular. The other students couldn't understand why he liked someone whom they considered inferior to them. So, to clear the matter up, Hadrat Junaid ﷺ said, "This student is the most respectful and intelligent amongst you, and I'm going to show you what he has that you all don't."

He then gave each one of them a chicken and a knife and said, "Find a place to slaughter these chickens where no-one else will see you."

So, every student went out, found an isolated area to carry out their slaughtering and returned back to the class, but the student who was liked by Hadrat Junaid ﷺ arrived with his chicken still alive.

Hadrat asked him, "Why didn't you slaughter it?"

He replied, "I couldn't find any place where I was not watched by Allah ﷻ, so I was forced to come back unsuccessful."

Hadrat Junaid ﷺ then turned to the class and said, "See? It's this quality he has in him that makes me like him so much." – *Tazkiratul-Auliya, Pg. 447*

Lesson If we truly grasped the fact that Allah ﷻ is seeing us at all times, we would try harder to not commit any sin in our lives.

107 – TEARS

Hadrat Abu Bakr Shibli ﷺ was once looking at a stick burning in his stove and noticed that while one end was on fire, the other was leaking water. He began to cry and said, "If you say that you burn with the desire (to meet Allah ﷻ) and are true in your claim, why don't your eyes ever pour?" – *Tazkiratul-Auliya, Pg. 427*

108 – SEEKING HELP

Some caravan-travelers were once about to leave for a long journey. For this reason, they presented themselves before Hadrat Abul-Hasan

Kharqaani ﷺ and said, "The road we are taking is dangerous. Teach us some dua that will safeguard us along the way."

He replied, "If you see any danger, mention my name."

The travelers didn't like this suggestion of his and later said amongst themselves, "*Must we mention his name and not Allah's ﷺ?!*"

Incidentally, during their journey, the group was confronted by some robbers who surrounded their caravan and began to loot them. One of the passengers, however, decided to take the name of Hadrat Abul-Hasan Kharqaani ﷺ, so he said, "O Abul-Hasan ﷺ, help us!"

As soon he said this, he turned invisible (while the robbers continued to loot everyone else).

When the robbers finally left the area, the man reappeared and was asked by his friends, "How were you saved? Where did you go?"

He then related the entire incident to them.

When the group returned from the journey, everyone went to Hadrat Abul-Hasan ﷺ and said, "Hadrat, what's the meaning of this?! We were all shouting for Allah ﷺ but were robbed while the one who called out for you was saved!"

The great Saint replied, "Brother, you call out to Allah ﷺ only by mere lip-service. I call out to Him from the *bottom* of my heart. From now on, mention my name so that I may call out to Allah ﷺ for you and so that you may be successful in your aims. Calling out to Allah ﷺ by way of mere formality even thousands of times will be of no benefit." – *Tazkiratul-Auliya, Pg. 632*

Lesson Help is ultimately and only from Allah ﷺ, but He has placed His Messengers ﷺ and Friends ﷺ on this earth as His intermediaries. This is the reason why we seek assistance from them (because through their friendship and special closeness to Allah ﷺ, we may attain His help faster). Allah ﷺ states in the Holy Quran, "O You who believe! Do your duty towards Allah ﷺ, seek the *wasilah* (i.e. mediation, way of approach) unto Him." [5]

109 – MAHMOOD GHAZNAWI ﷺ ON THE DOORSTEP OF ABUL-HASAN KHARQAANI ﷺ

The king Mahmood Ghaznawi ﷺ was once informed of a miracle by Hadrat Abul-Hasan Kharqaani ﷺ and wished to meet with him. For some time, he tried inviting the great Saint to his residence in Ghazni but was constantly denied his presence.

In the end, he decided *he* would go and see him. And so, after reaching the city of Kharqaan and pitching a regal tent on the outskirts of the city, the king dispatched someone to the great Saint with the following message, "The current ruler has left his city of Ghazni for Kharqaan to meet with you. He will be forever grateful if you trouble yourself for just a short while to come and see him."

He also told the messenger that if Hadrat Abul-Hasan ؓ wishes to exempt himself from even this invitation, he should be reminded of the following verse of the Holy Quran,

اطیعوا الله و اطیعوا الرسول و اولی الامر منکم

"Obey Allah ﷻ and His Messenger ﷺ and those of authority amongst you."
– Surah Nisā (4), Verse 59

When the messenger delivered the message and was told by Hadrat Abul-Hasan ؓ that he wouldn't come, he read the verse he was ordered to and said to him, "According to this, you are obligated to meet with the king."

Hadrat Abul-Hasan ؓ replied, "It's due to that first injunction – 'Obey Allah ﷻ' – that I cannot come. Even regarding the second injunction, I have yet to fulfill many commands of the Holy Prophet ﷺ. We'll be given chances to obey kings our entire lives, but we cannot obey our Lord for even a moment."

When the messenger delivered this fair reply to Sultaan Mahmood Ghaznawi ؓ, the king stood up and told his fellow travelers, "Abul-Hasan ؓ has denied our invitation again. It's time we go and meet with him."

Before leaving, the king wished to test the Divinely-bestowed intuition of the great Saint and dressed his servant Ayaaz with his regal clothes (even going as far as placing the crown on his head!). He also put on Ayaaz's servant-garment and dressed his female-servants in the garbs of men. All then left for Hadrat's cottage in this disguise.

When their caravan reached the place, Hadrat Abul-Hasan Kharqaani ؓ came out and paid no attention to Ayaaz (the servant in the king's clothing). Instead, he turned to Sultaan Mahmood ؓ (who was standing behind Ayaaz) and said, "Take these women away."

After the female-servants were removed from the gathering, Hadrat Abul-Hasan ؓ said, "You came with quite a trap."

The king replied, "A trap which has been proven as false as you are rare."

Hadrat Abul-Hasan ؓ then offered him a piece of dry bread as a relic of a Saint (رحه), and in response, Mahmood Ghaznawi ؓ offered him a few bags of gold coins. He then placed the piece of bread he was given in his mouth.

Suddenly, the bread got caught inside the delicate throat of the king and he began to start coughing. At that moment, Hadrat Abul-Hasan Kharqaani ؓ pointed to the bags of gold and said, "Mahmood ؓ! Food from the prophets won't go down your throat just as how the money in these bags taken from the inheritance of Pharoah won't go down this beggar's throat."

After much persistence from the king to take the gold, Hadrat Abul-Hasan ؓ continued to refuse the offer and finally said, "I don't need it. Give it to its rightful owners, the people who it belonged to in the first place."

Hearing this, the king became even more captivated by the Saint and sincerely accepted him as a Friend of Allah ﷻ from then on. – *Tazkiratul-Auliya, Pg. 638*

110 – TURNING THE TIDE

As king, Sultaan Mahmood Ghaznawi ؓ had great respect for Hadrat Abul-Hasan Kharqaani ؓ and would always present himself in his service. On one occasion, he was even granted a garment worn by the great Saint.

Once, during the battle of Sumnāth, the king's army started showing signs of weakness and began to drain their weapon supply. All could see that the battle was quickly going into the hands of the enemy.

After losing all hope in material strength, Sultaan Mahmood ؓ decided to seek spiritual assistance and immediately separated himself from the battlefield. Once he was alone, he read two rakaats nafl Salaah and made the following supplication (with the garment given to him by Hadrat Abul-Hasan Kharqaani ؓ in his hands), "O Allah ﷻ! In honour of your beloved servant, the wearer of this garment, grant me victory in this war."

Immediately, the king found the tide of war turning and very courageously re-entered the conflict, attributing this change of consequences to the dua he just made.

Lesson Where physical might ends, spiritual might begins – performing duties not even the sword is capable of. This is what can be carried out with the assistance of just the *clothes* of the Friends of Allah ﷻ, nevermind the Saints themselves!

85

Also, if a mere garment worn by a Saint can be so favored by Allah ﷻ, why shouldn't one who constantly keeps himself with His Friends ﷻ not gain any favour himself?

And, if these followers of the Holy Prophet ﷺ are respected in the Divine court to this extent, what can now be said of the status of the *Beloved* of Allah, Sayyiduna Muhammadur-Rasoolullah ﷺ?!

111 – THE LEADER OF PROPHETS ﷺ WITH SHAIKH ABDUL-QADIR JILAANI ﷺ

Shaikh Abdul-Qadir Jilaani ﷺ states, "I was once visited by the Holy Prophet ﷺ before Zohr Salaah, while I was awake. He asked me, "Why don't you lecture?"

I replied, "O Rasoolullah ﷺ, how can I lecture while so many eloquent speakers are present in Baghdad?"

He told me to open my mouth and then placed his blessed saliva inside it seven times, saying afterwards, "Now you may begin speaking without fear."

So, after performing Zohr Salaah, I sat to begin my first lecture and found that before I could even speak, people were beginning to gather around me (and even created some congestion). Hadrat Ali ﷺ then emerged from the crowd and asked, "Why haven't you started yet?"

I replied, "I have no courage to speak in front of so many people."

Hearing this, he ordered me to open my mouth and then placed his blessed saliva inside it *six* times. When I asked him why he did so, he replied, "ادبا مع رسول الله ﷺ In respect of the Messenger of Allah ﷺ. If I had done it seven times, it would have been an action seeking equality with him, which is disrespectful. For that, I did it one less time."

Shaikh Abdul-Qadir Jilaani ﷺ continues, "All the veils were then lifted off me and I began to deliver an honorable sermon." – *Bahjatul-Asraar, Pg. 25*

Lesson After their demise, the prophets are immediately returned to life and meet with their followers even until today (be it in a dream or physically in this world).

We also see that the Holy Prophet's ﷺ saliva is a source of knowledge and a treasure of secrets. In fact, the abovementioned two qualities are not only shown for the Prophet ﷺ but even for his Sahaabah ﷺ. How then can we, whose tongues are the cause of so much sin, claim to be equal to these illustrious individuals?

Shaikh Abdul-Qadir Jilaani ﷺ was once delivering a lecture to a gathering when it began to rain. Seeing the people starting to leave, he looked up to the sky and said, "انا اجمع و انت تفرق O Allah ﷻ, I have gathered them for Your remembrance and You are taking them away."

The rain immediately ceased over the crowd (but continued around them)! – *Bahjatul-Asraar, Pg. 75*

Lesson The wish of the Friends of Allah ﷻ is also the wish of Allah ﷻ (due to His special love for them and the fact that they will never ask for something against His pleasure).

Supplement In this very book, it's also stated that other Saints related this miracle of Shaikh Abdul-Qadir Jilaani ﷺ when caught in rain and found it to cease at once.

113 – THE TIGRIS RIVER STOPS OVERFLOWING

The Tigris River was once beginning to overflow, and so in panic, the people went to Shaikh Abdul-Qadir Jilaani ﷺ and sought his assistance in this matter.

The Saint took his blessed staff, walked towards the river and said when he reached it (striking his staff into the ground), "الى ههنا Until here!"

The river then receded and continued to flow until only where Shaikh Abdul-Qadir ﷺ had ordered it to! – *Bahjatul-Asraar, Pg. 75*

Lesson We can't even stop water flowing in our drains, but even *rivers* are within the control of the Friends of Allah ﷻ!

114 – THE KNOWLEDGE OF SHAIKH ABDUL-QADIR JILAANI ﷺ

Shaikh Abdul-Qadir Jilaani ﷺ once said, "If Shariah (Islamic Law) wasn't stopping me, I'd inform you of everything you eat and store in your homes. You are all like glass bottles in front of me. I see both your internal and external states." – *Bahjatul-Asraar, Pg. 24*

Lesson Nothing on this earth is hidden from the Friends of Allah ﷺ. Even the King of Saints, Hadrat Abu Bakr Siddique ﷺ, informed his wife

(Sayyidah Bint Khaarija ؓ) that she was pregnant with a girl before his demise.

115 – THE CHIEF THIEF

Even at a young age, Shaikh Abdul-Qadir Jilaani ؓ showed great interest in acquiring Islamic knowledge and one day said to his mother, "Give me permission to go to Baghdad and become a scholar."

She replied, "You may go," and then handed him 40 gold coins (which Shaikh Abdul-Qadir Jilaani ؓ sealed in a purse and fastened to his belt).

Before he could leave, his mother also advised him to always speak the truth.

Shaikh Abdul-Qadir Jilaani ؓ then left his home with other travelers in a caravan towards Baghdad.

Along the way, they reached a remote area and were suddenly surrounded by a group of thieves on horseback who began to loot the passengers onboard. One of them approached the young boy (Shaikh Abdul-Qadir Jilaani ؓ) and asked him if he had anything of value. He replied, "Yes, forty gold coins."

When the robber asked him where they were, he answered, "Here in this waist-belt."

Thinking that he was merely joking, the thief turned around and walked away.

When the same reply was given to several other thieves, they began to get suspicious of the boy and took him to their leader, who asked him, "Boy! Do you have anything to give?"

Hadrat Shaikh Abdul-Qadir ؓ again replied, "Yes, forty gold coins."

"Where are they?"

"In this belt of mine."

The leader then began to search the belt, and after indeed finding 40 gold coins inside, he asked the Saint in surprise, "Why didn't you try to hide this from us?!"

Shaikh Abdul-Qadir Jilaani ؓ replied, "My mother took an oath from me that I will never lie, so I'm not breaking that promise now and never will."

Hearing this, the chief let out a shout and began to cry, saying, "How unfortunate that a little boy can show so much regard to a promise made to his mother whereas I can't even be faithful to my promise made to Allah ﷻ?! Boy, let out your hand."

He then repented to Allah ﷻ on the hand of Shaikh Abdul-Qadir Jilaani ؓ before turning to his men and saying, "You can all leave. You have nothing else to do with me now."

They replied, "You were always our leader, and so we'll continue to stay with you. Even now, we make tauba from our ways just like you."

All then returned the goods to the travelers and lived the rest of their lives as people in fear of Allah ﷻ. – *Bahjatul-Asraar, Pg. 57*

Lesson The Friends of Allah ؓ do not lie – and through this honesty, many astray individuals can be corrected. Even as a child, Shaikh Abdul-Qadir Jilaani ؓ was proof of this quality.

116 – THE MOON OF RAMADAAN

A dispute once arose concerning the sighting of the moon supposed to commence the month of Ramadaan. Some said that it had already appeared while others said that it didn't. The mother of Shaikh Abdul-Qadir Jilaani ؓ settled this by saying, "Since my baby (Shaikh Abdul-Qadir ؓ) was born, he never drank milk during any day of Ramadaan. Today too, he stopped drinking. That's how I know the moon appeared last night."

Later, upon investigation, it was found out that the moon did indeed appear the night before! – *Bahjatul-Asraar, Pg. 79*

Lesson Those who are born the Friends of Allah ؓ show signs of piety even in their childhood.

117 – "STAND, BY THE COMMAND OF ALLAH ﷻ!"

A woman once brought her child to the great Saint, Shaikh Abdul-Qadir Jilaani ؓ, and said, "This boy of mine is very fond of you. I'll leave him here for training so that he may gain blessings and benefit as he grows up."

She then left him there and proceeded back to her home.

A few days later, the woman returned to meet her son and found him weak and thin, eating dry bread. She then proceeded to Shaikh Abdul-Qadir Jilaani ؓ and saw *him* eating *cooked chicken*!

In shock, she asked the great Saint, "You're eating chicken but you're giving my son dry bread?!"

Hearing this, Shaikh Abdul-Qadir Jilaani ﵁ placed the chicken-bones into his hand and said, "قومى باذن الله Stand, by the command of Allah ﷻ!"
The chicken then came alive and began to move about!

Shaikh Abdul-Qadir Jilaani ﵁ then looked at the woman and said, "When your son can do this, he can eat whatever he wants." – *Bahjatul-Asraar, Pg. 65*

Lesson Just as how Hadrat Esa ﵊ could give life to the dead by the command of Allah ﷻ, so do the Friends of Allah ﵁ have this quality in them too.

118 – THE BIRD'S HEAD

Shaikh Abdul-Qadir Jilaani ﵁ was once delivering a lecture when a bird of prey began circling and making noise above him. He looked up to the sky and said, "يا ريح خذى راس هذه الحداة Wind! Grab the head of that bird!"
At once, the bird jerked in the air and fell to the ground in two pieces (its head separated from its body).

After the lecture, the Saint picked up the two body parts and placed them together, saying, "Bismillahir-Rahmanir-Raheem." The bird then immediately came back to life and flew away. This miracle was seen by the entire gathering. – *Bahjatul-Asraar, Pg. 65*

119 – FORTY-EIGHT QUESTIONS*

Hadrat Bā-Yazeed Bustaami ﵁ was once performing ibaadat in serenity when he heard a voice from the unseen saying, "Bā-Yazeed. Put on the clothes of a priest and go to the temple of Sam'aan to join the people in their celebration."

The Saint immediately sought refuge from Allah ﷻ for such an odd thought and continued in his worship.

That night, he was given the same order in a dream and instantly woke up in a fright. The voice was then heard again, saying, "Bā-Yazeed, don't worry. This will incur no sin on you. You are a friend of Mine and from amongst the good people. Put on the clothes and go to the temple."

So, Hadrat Bā-Yazeed ﵁ got up, wore the clothes he was instructed to and joined the idol-worshippers in their gathering.

At that time, the crowd was awaiting their head priest who they'd come to listen to. When he finally arrived, he seemed to have something preventing him from speaking and was asked by everyone, "Why aren't you saying anything?"

The priest replied, "It's not that someone is stopping me from speaking. It's that there's a follower of Muhammad sitting amongst you somewhere who came to put our religion under trial."

All responded, "Who is he?! Tell us so we can kill him!"

The priest replied, "We'll fight him with proofs and evidence of our beliefs, not with our hands."

He then stood up and shouted, "Muslim! I give you the oath of Muhammad! Stand so that we may see you!"

When the great Saint stood up (praising and glorifying Allah ﷻ), the priest continued, "I'm going to ask you a few questions. If you answer them correctly, we'll become your followers. If not, we'll kill you here and now."

Hadrat Bā-Yazeed ؓ replied, "I understand. Ask what you wish."

The priest began,

1. What's the one thing nothing else is similar to?
2. What are the two things that have no third?
3. What are the three things that have no fourth?
4. What are the four things that have no fifth?
5. What are the five things that have no sixth?
6. What are the six things that have no seventh?
7. What are the seven things that have no eighth?
8. What are the eight things that have no ninth?
9. What are the nine things that have no tenth?
10. What are the ten complete things?
11. What are eleven?
12. What are twelve?
13. What are thirteen?
14. What are the fourteen things that speak to Allah ﷻ?
15. Who were the ones that lied but were sent to Jannah?
16. Who were the ones that spoke the truth but were sent to Jahannam?
17. What is ذاريات ذروا Zaariyaati-Zarwaa?[6]
18. What is حاملات وقرا Haamilaati-Waqraa?[7]
19. What is جاريات يسرا Jaariyaati-Yusraa?[8]

20. What is مقسمات امرا Muqassimaati-Amraa?[9]
21. What breathes but has no soul?
22. Which grave went to its inhabitant and carried him around?
23. Which water came from neither the sky nor the earth?
24. Who or what are the four that are neither human, jinn, angel, from the spine of any father nor from the womb of any mother?
25. Who committed the first murder?
26. What did Allah ﷻ create then hate?
27. What did Allah ﷻ create then make great?
28. Who are the most respected women?
29. Which are the most respected rivers?
30. Which is the most respected mountain?
31. Which is the most respected four-legged animal?
32. Which is the most respected month?
33. What is the Calamity (الطامة)?[10]
34. Which is the tree that has twelve branches, each branch containing thirty leaves and each leaf containing five buds, two of which are in the shade while the other three are in sunlight?
35. What performed Hajj and made Tawaaf even though it was not obligated to and had no soul?
36. How many Prophets did Allah ﷻ create?
37. How many of them were Messengers?
38. What are the four waters that are different in colour and taste but are all from the same source?
39. What is Qitmeer (قطمير)?
40. What is Subd (سبد) and Lubd (لبد)?
41. What is Rumm (رم) and Tumm (طم)?
42. What does a dog say when it barks?
43. What does a donkey say when it brays?
44. What does a horse say when it neighs?
45. What does a frog say when it croaks?
46. What does a shell say when it's blown?
47. Which nation did Allah ﷻ send revelation to that wasn't of man, jinn or angel?
48. And finally, where does the night go during the day, and where does the day go during the night?"

When the priest was done, Hadrat Bā-Yazeed Bustaami ﷺ asked him, "Do you have any more questions?"
He replied, "No."

The Saint then asked, "If I answer these questions, will you bring faith on Allah ﷻ and His Messenger ﷺ?"

All replied that they would.

Hadrat Bā-Yazeed Bustaami ؓ then said, "O Allah ﷻ! Be witness to what they say. Now, priest, here are your answers,

1. The one thing nothing else is similar to is Allah ﷻ.

2. The two things that have no third are night & day, as stated by Allah ﷻ, "و جعلنا الليل و النهار ايتين" We have made the night and the day as two (of Our) signs." [11]

3. The three things that have no fourth are the Arsh, Kūrsi and Qalam.

4. The four things that have no fifth are the Four Books: the Torah, Zabur, Injeel & Quran.

5. The five things that have no sixth are the Five Daily Salaah compulsory on all Muslims.

6. The six things that have no seventh are the six days mentioned by Allah ﷻ, "و لقد خلقنا السموت و الارض و ما بينهما فى ستة ايام" And We indeed created the Heavens, the Earth and what is between them in six days." [12]

7. The seven things that have no eighth are the Seven Heavens, "خلق سبع سموت طباقا" He created the Seven Heavens one above the other." [13]

8. The eight things that have no ninth are the eight angels appointed to hold up the Arsh, "و يحمل عرش ربك فوقهم يومئذ ثمنية" And the eight of them will on that Day hold up the Throne above them." [14]

9. The nine things that have no tenth are the nine men who caused mischief on the earth, "و كان فى المدينة تسعة رهط يفسدون فى الارض و لا يصلحون" And there was in a city nine men of a family who made mischief in the land and would not reform." [15]

10. The ten complete things are the ten obligations of Hajj, "فصيام ثلاثة ايام فى الحج و سبعة اذا رجعتم تلك عشرة كاملة" He should fast three days during the Hajj and seven days in all." [16]

93

11. The eleven things are the eleven brothers of Hadrat Yusuf عليه السلام.

12. The twelve things are the twelve months of the year.

13. The thirteen things are the thirteen things Hadrat Yusuf عليه السلام saw in his dream, "انى رايت احد عشر كوكبا و الشمس و القمر Indeed I saw eleven stars, the sun and the moon." [17]

14. The fourteen things that speak to Allah ﷻ are the seven Heavens and seven Earths, "فقال لها و للارض ائتنا طوعا او كرها قالتا أتينا طائعين He said to them, "Come to it, willingly or unwillingly." They replied, "We do come, in willing obedience." [18]

15. The people that lied but were sent to Jannah were the brothers of Hadrat Yusuf عليه السلام who said that their brother was attacked by an animal, "و جاءوا على قميصه بدم كذب They stained his shirt with false blood." [19]

16. The people that spoke the truth but were sent to Jahannam were the Christians and Jews when they argued amongst themselves, " و قالت اليهود ليست النصرى على شئ و قالت النصارى ليست اليهود على شئ The Jews say, 'The Christians have naught (to stand) upon', and the Christians say, 'The Jews have naught (to stand) upon.'" [20]

17. *Zaariyaati-Zarwaa* are the four winds.

18. *Haamilaati-Waqraa* are the clouds.

19. *Jaariyaati-Yusraa* are ships traveling on rivers.

20. *Muqassimaati-Amraa* are the angels who distribute sustenance on the 15th night of Shabaan.

21. The thing that breathes but has no soul is the morning.

22. The grave that went to its inhabitant and carried him around was the fish of Hadrat Yunus عليه السلام.

23. The water that came from neither the sky nor the earth was the sweat of the horse that Bilqees sent to Hadrat Sulaiman ﷺ in a bottle.

24. The four that are neither human, jinn, angel, from the spine of any father nor from the womb of any mother are 1) Hadrat Adam ﷺ, 2) Sayyidah Hawa ﷺ, 3) the ram of Hadrat Ismail ﷺ, 4) and the camel of Hadrat Salih ﷺ.

25. The first murder was committed by Qābīl against his brother Hābīl.

26. The thing that Allah ﷻ created then hated was the sound of the donkey, "ان انكر الاصوات لصوت الحمير The harshest of sounds without doubt is the braying of an ass." [21]

27. The thing that Allah ﷻ created then made great was the deception of a woman, "ان كيدكن عظيم Truly mighty is your (i.e. you women's) snare." [22]

28. The most respected women are the Mothers of Mankind, Sayyidah Khadija ؓ, Sayyidah Aisha ؓ, Sayyidah Aa'sia ؓ and Sayyidah Maryam bint Imraan ؓ.

29. The most respected rivers are the Jaxartes, Oxus, Euphrates and Nile.

30. The most respected mountain is Mount Toor.

31. The most respected four-legged animal is the horse.

32. The most respected month is Ramadaan.

33. The Calamity (الطامة) is the Day of Judgment.

34. The tree that has twelve branches, each branch containing thirty leaves and each leaf containing five buds, two of which are in the shade while the other three are in sunlight is *a year*. The twelve branches are its months and the thirty leaves are its days. The five buds on each leaf are the Five Daily Salaah, two of which are read at night while the other three are read in the day.

95

35. The thing that performed Hajj and made Tawaaf even though it was not obligated to and had no soul was the ark of Hadrat Nuh عَلَيْهِ السَّلَامُ.

36. Allah عَزَّوَجَلَّ created more than 100,000 Prophets…

37. Of which only 313 were Messengers.

38. The four waters that are different in colour and taste but are all from the same source are the four waters which emanate from the eyes, ears, nose and mouth. The water of the eyes is salty, the water of the ears is bitter, the water of the nose is sour and the water of the mouth is sweet. All are from the brain.

39. 'Qitmeer' is the outer-layer of the skin.

40. 'Subd' is the hair of sheep and 'Lubd' is the hair of goats.

41. 'Rumm' and 'Tumm' are the nations that existed before Hadrat Adam عَلَيْهِ السَّلَامُ.

42. When a dog barks, it's saying, "How unfortunate are the inmates of Jahannam with the anger of their Lord upon them!?"

43. When a donkey brays, it's seeing Shaitaan and saying, "لعن الله العشار."

44. When a horse neighs, it's saying, "May Allah عَزَّوَجَلَّ protect me when lies spread and men become intimate with men."

45. When a frog croaks, it's saying, "سبحان المعبود فى البرارى و القفار سبحان للملك الجبار".

46. When a shell is blown, it's saying, "سبحان الله حقا حقا انظر يا ابن آدم فى هذه الدنيا غربا و شرقا ما ترى فيها احد يبقى Glory truly be to Allah عَزَّوَجَلَّ! Look at the easts and the wests of this world, O son of Adam عَلَيْهِ السَّلَامُ, and know that all will one day cease to exist."

47. The nation that Allah عَزَّوَجَلَّ sent revelation to that wasn't of man, jinn or angel was the bee, "و اوحى ربك الى النحل And Your Lord sent revelation to the bee." [23]

48. As for where night and day go when any one of them is not with us, they both hide themselves in the vessel of Allah's ﷻ knowledge."

After giving these answers, Hadrat Bā-Yazeed Bustaami ؓ asked, "Are there any more questions?"

All replied, "No."

He then said, "Now you tell me: what is the key to the skies and the Heavens?"

Hearing this, the priest turned to his followers and shouted, "Keep quiet! Don't say anything to him!"

The Saint continued, "You asked me so many questions and I answered them all. I'm only asking you one, yet you're not answering it. Are you unable to?"

The crowd replied, "Yes, we cannot answer it."

All then turned to their priest and asked him, "Do you also not know the answer?"

He replied, "I know the answer, but I'm afraid you all won't agree with me."

They responded, "Of course we'll believe in you! You're our leader!"

The priest then gave in and said, "The key to the skies and the Heavens is the *Kalima for Muslims*: لا اله الا الله محمد رسول الله There is none worthy of worship but Allah ﷻ, Muhammad ﷺ is His Messenger."

Hearing this, the *entire* gathering then read the Kalima of Islam and became Muslims! They even broke down their temple and turned it into a musjid. As this occurred, Hadrat Bā-Yazeed Bustaami ؓ heard the voice from the unseen saying to him, "You wore one of their uniforms for Us, so We tore 500 of them for you." – *Raudul-Riyaheen, Pg. 40*

120 – THE BIRD & THE BLIND SNAKE

A group of thieves once stumbled upon an area that had three date trees and decided to rest beneath them. (The dates on one of the trees were dry while those of the other two were ripe.)

As they lay down, their leader noticed something peculiar – a bird kept flying between the dry date tree and another. Out of curiosity, he got up and climbed one of them to see what was going on.

As he got higher, he noticed that the longest branch of the tree had a blind snake coiled around it with its mouth wide-open. The bird had been bringing dates to it from the other tree and placing it in his mouth.

The thief was astonished upon seeing this and said, "O Allah ﷻ! You appointed a bird to deliver sustenance to such a wicked creation! How can I, being from the best of creation (i.e. Man), be content with myself as a thief?"

He immediately heard a voice from the unseen saying, "The doors of My mercy are always open. Even if you make tauba now, I will accept it."

The chief then burst into tears, descended to the ground and said (after breaking his sword), "O Allah ﷻ! I repent from every sin of mine! I ask You to accept it."

The voice answered, "We have accepted it."

During this commotion, the other thieves woke up and asked him, "What's happening?"

After being informed of the entire incident, they too began crying and thereafter repented from their ways.

Some time later, the group decided to go for Hajj and passed by a small village along the way. An old, blind lady emerged from one of the houses and mentioned a certain name to them, asking, "Do you know this person?"

The leader stepped forward and replied, "Yes, I'm that person."

She then entered her house and came out with a bundle of clothes saying, "My son passed away some time ago. In the last few nights, I've continuously seen the Holy Prophet ﷺ in a dream telling me to give his old clothes to a certain person who'll be passing through the village soon. Since you're that person, these clothes are now yours."

The leader then went into a state of ecstasy, put on the clothes, and proceeded to Makkah Mukarramah to eventually be counted amongst the pious. – *Raudul-Riyaheen, Pg. 126*

Lesson No matter how many sins a person may have committed in his life, he will always be forgiven – as long as he repents to Allah ﷻ with a sincere heart.

We also learn that the Holy Prophet ﷺ is aware of every action of his Ummah and is pleased when they repent from their bad ways.

121 – AUTHORITY OVER A LION

Hadrat Sufyaan Thauri ؓ narrates, "Hadrat Shaibaan ؓ and I were once walking through a jungle towards Makkah to perform Hajj when we saw a lion along the way.

I asked him, "What do we do now?"
He simply replied, "Don't worry," and continued moving closer towards it.
When he reached it, he grabbed the ear of the lion and said, "Move out of our path."
The lion immediately woke up, wagged its tail like a dog and walked away!
I said to him, "That was incredible!"
He replied, "If I didn't fear being popular, I would've loaded our goods onto its back and taken it with us to Makkah." – *Raudul-Riyaheen, Pg. 128*

Lesson When the Friends of Allah ﷻ obey and fear their Lord, everything in His creation begins to obey and fear them. How then can people who are scared of even *insects* hope to think of themselves as equal to the Saints?!

122 – Ya Lateef ﷻ!

A pious man narrates, "I was once in tremendous difficulty and even began to fear for my life. Not knowing what to do, I eventually decided to go to Makkah and perform Hajj even though I had no money to travel by caravan and hardly any to travel by foot.
On the fourth day of my journey, I began to grow weak due to hunger and thirst and thought that I may well have been experiencing the last few moments of my life. There wasn't even a tree in sight for me to sit beneath, so I sat on the road facing the *qibla* (thinking that if I *did* die here, at least it would be while facing the Kaaba). Tiredness ultimately overtook me and I eventually fell off to sleep.
In my dream, I saw a handsome man full of Noor approach me and shake my hands, saying, "Good news. You will soon reach Makkah and present yourself at the Rauda of the Beloved Prophet ﷺ."
I asked him, "Who are you?"
He replied, "I'm Khidr عليه السلام."
I then requested him to make dua for me, after which he said, "Learn this dua and read it three times,

يا لطيفا بخلقه ، يا عليما بخلقه ، يا خبيرا بخلقه ، الطف لى يا لطيف يا عليم يا خبير

Ya Lateefan-Bi'khalqihee, Ya Aleeman-Bi'khalqihee, Ya Khabeeram-Bi'khalqihee. Ultuf lee Ya Lateef Ya Aleem Ya Khabeer

"O You Who is kind towards His creation! O You Who is informed of His creation! Be kind towards me, O Allah ﷻ."

"Take it as a gift from us. Insha-Allah, whenever you're faced with any danger, calamity or trouble, read it three times and the problem will go away."

As soon as he said this, someone woke me up and asked, "Excuse me, have you seen my son?"

It was a man on a camel. I replied that I didn't and asked him what had happened. He explained that he and his son were both traveling together on their way to perform Hajj when they became separated. He then asked, "Where are you going?"

I replied that I was also on my way to perform Hajj, and so I was requested by him to ride along and was even provided with enough food and water to replenish myself.

Fortunately, we passed by a caravan soon afterwards and found his son sitting inside.

When we reached Makkah, someone handed me a bag of coins as a gift, providing me with enough money for the journey back. I later visited the sacred Rauda in Madina and eventually left the two cities to head back home. Alhamdulillah, upon my return, I also found that the problem I'd been previously afflicted with was solved." – *Raudul-Riyaaheen, Pg. 175*

Lesson If someone turns to Allah ﷻ during a severe difficulty, Allah ﷻ may send one of His Friends to assist him if He so wishes.

We also come to know that the abovementioned dua has proven helpful and should be memorized by all.

123 – GUEST OR HOST?

There was a Saint who chose to live on a hill so that he could focus more of his time towards the worship of Allah ﷻ. He narrates, "I once came down on the day of Eid to read Salaah with everyone and then headed back to where I was staying. Upon my arrival, I found a man full of Noor sitting there reading Salaah with no sign of travel on his clothes. I stared at him in bewilderment and thought, 'Who's this man? How and when did he come here? Nevertheless, he's my guest and today's the day of Eid. I should give him something to eat…but I don't have anything.'

When the man turned his head in Salaam (to end his Salaah), he looked at me and said, "Don't worry about me. I'll be seen to by the One Who provides sustenance. If, however, you *do* feel the need to offer me something, bring me a cup of water."

So, I proceeded to my water-container and was surprised to find fresh, hot bread and curry placed near it (as if they'd just been prepared). This startled me even more so, but my mysterious guest comforted me by saying, "فان لله عبادا اينما كانوا وحلوا ما ارادوا There are some servants of Allah ﷻ who, whenever they want something, they get it."

He then instructed me to sit and eat with him. When we were finished, he made Salaam to me and then disappeared. – *Raudul-Riyaaheen, Pg. 178*

Lesson The Friends of Allah ﷻ are above ordinary worshippers and are granted whatever they desire by their Creator.

124 – THE INTELLIGENCE OF A 'FOOL'

The Islamic ruler Hadrat Haroon Rashid was once traveling to perform Hajj and stopped in the city of Kufa for a few days along the way. After his stay, as he was leaving in his regal procession, he came across Hadrat Bahlool 'Majnoon' ؓ (a Saint so engrossed and distracted in the remembrance of Allah ﷻ that people regarded him as a madman due to his unconventionality) and was told by him, "Leader of the Muslims! Listen to this Hadith before you leave. Hadrat Abdullah Aamiri ؓ states that the Holy Prophet ﷺ was once performing Hajj and traveled modestly on the plains of Mina with nothing but a camel and a simple saddle beneath him, showing no signs of arrogance or majesty. O Haroon Rashid! You should also travel in this manner."

The ruler began to cry upon hearing this and said, "Bahlool ؓ, give me more advice."

The Saint continued, "When Allah ﷻ grants someone wealth and beauty, He will admit that individual amongst His friends *if* the wealth given is spent in His path and the beauty given is not exploited."

Haroon Rashid then said, "You please me, O Bahlool ؓ. If there's anyone you owe any money to, tell me so that I may pay him for you."

Hadrat Bahlool ؓ answered, "How can debt be repaid with debt? It would be better to owe nothing to anyone but Allah ﷻ and constantly live to repay Him as His slave."

Haroon Rashid then asked, "Okay. Do you wish for land instead?"

He replied, *"O Leader of the Muslims, when we are both servants of Allah ﷻ, how can He remember one and forsake the other?"* – *Raudul-Riyaaheen, Pg. 31*

Lesson Even though certain Friends of Allah ﷻ may seem as madmen to the ordinary person, they are in fact treasures of the wisdom of Allah ﷻ and adorn the world with their insightful teachings.

We also learn that previous Islamic rulers had tremendous fear of Allah ﷻ and great respect for His Beloved Messenger's ﷺ narrations (احاديث) and teachings.

125 – A BAG OF CLOTHES

Hadrat Abul-Husain Noori ﷺ once lit a few coals in his stove and instructed his female servant to bring him some milk which he could warm up and have with his bread. As he began to eat, the servant noticed that his hands were still black (from touching the coals) and thought to herself, "This man is supposedly a Friend of Allah ﷻ yet he has no concern for cleanliness."

She then exited the house to rest. While outside, a woman came up to her, grabbed her and angrily accused her of having stolen a bag of clothes she'd just lost. Both then proceeded to the nearby jail to have the matter solved.

When Hadrat Abul-Husain Noori ﷺ came to know of this, he too proceeded to the jailhouse and said to the policeman when he reached it, "This woman is without fault. Let her go."

The policeman asked, "Can you prove this?"

He replied, "See for yourself."

At that moment, another woman (from the accuser's home) entered the jail and said that she had found the missing bag. So, the servant was free to go.

Before she could leave, Hadrat Abul-Husain Noori ﷺ met with his servant and asked her, "Will you say again that the Friends of Allah ﷺ have no concern for cleanliness?"

She replied, "Huzoor, forgive me!" – *Raudul-Riyaaheen, Pg. 126*

Lesson Never look with contempt at the actions of the Friends of Allah ﷺ lest you wish to be put into difficulty (should you earn their anger).

126 – A JEWEL IN RAGS

Hadrat Shafeeq Balkhi ﷺ narrates, "I once left my home to perform Hajj and reached the area of Qādisiyya along the way. While there, I noticed a man with beautiful features and simple clothes sitting on one of the pathways and thought, "This man's supposedly pious yet he chooses to burden people by blocking their path."

As I neared him, the man looked at me and said, "Shafeeq ﷺ,

اجتنبوا كثيرا من الظن ان بعض الظن اثم

*"Save yourselves from many presumptions. Indeed
some presumptions become sins."*
– Surah Hujarāt (49), Verse 12

He then got up and walked away.

Since he knew the thoughts of my heart, I decided to follow the man and seek his forgiveness (not wanting to insult someone who may be a Friend of Allah ﷻ). I eventually found him shivering and crying in Salaah and decided to sit and wait until he was finished.

When he was done, he turned to me again and said, "Shafeeq ﷺ, read this verse of the Holy Quran, "انى لغفار لمن تاب و امن و عمل صالحا‏ Indeed I am He that forgives, again and again, those who repent, believe and do good deeds."[24]

After that, he turned around and walked away once more (this time disappearing for good).

Days later, during the Hajj, I saw him again in Mina sitting on a well saying, "O Allah ﷻ! I'm in need of water but this well has no bucket."

The water inside immediately began to flow upwards until it reached him. He then poured some of it into a vessel, made wudhu with it and began to read his Salaah. When he was finished, he placed a handful of sand into the container, shook it, and then drank some of the water that was left inside.

I came forward, made Salaam to him and said, "Show me a portion of the favour that Allah ﷻ has shown you."

In response, the Saint handed the vessel to me and told me to drink from it. I did…and by Allah ﷻ! It was the sweetest thing I'd ever tasted! I swear, even until today, I haven't forgotten its taste.

He then left me once again and disappeared.

I saw him a few more times after that: reading Salaah at night in the Haram and being respectfully greeted by people the day after. After asking some people who he was, they replied that he was the grandson of Hadrat Zainul-Aabideen ﷺ, Hadrat Musa ibn Ja'far Saadiq ﷺ. – *Raudul-Riyaaheen, Pg. 59*

Lesson Even though he was a close descendant of the Prophet ﷺ, Hadrat Musa ibn Ja'far Saadiq ﷺ never deterred himself from the worship of Allah

صلى الله عليه وسلم. How then can ordinary people like us feel no remorse in the 'only-what-is-Islamically-necessary' lives we live every day?

127 – THE BEGGAR OF THE HARAM

Hadrat Abu Saeed Kharaaz رضى الله عنه narrates, "I once saw someone in the Haram begging on a torn piece of sheet and thought to myself, "It's people like this that trouble those who pass by."
As soon as this came to mind, the beggar looked up towards me and said,

ان الله يعلم ما فى انفسكم فاحذروه
"Indeed Allah سبحانه وتعالى is aware of what's inside you, so fear Him."
– Surah Baqarah (2), Verse 235

I then repented from my statement, and the man then smiled and read the following,

هو الذى يقبل التوبة عن عباده و يعفو عن السيات
"He (Allah سبحانه وتعالى) accepts the tauba of his servants and forgives sins."
– Surah Shura (42), Verse 25

– Raudul-Riyaaheen, Pg. 59

Lesson Our inner desires and intentions are not hidden from the pious servants of Allah سبحانه وتعالى. How then can His Beloved Prophet صلى الله عليه وسلم not be endowed with these qualities too?

128 – A MYSTERIOUS BOY

Hadrat Sahl ibn Abdullah رضى الله عنه narrates, "I once went to the Jaami Musjid to read Jumaa Salaah and found it full of people, so I sat wherever I could and saw a young boy wearing simple, woollen clothes (with a strong fragrance emanating from him) sitting to my right. He asked me, "Sahl رضى الله عنه, how are you?"
I replied, "Alhamdulillah," but was surprised by this since I had no idea who he was.
A short while later, I felt a sudden urge to relieve myself (to such an extent that even sitting became difficult) but couldn't leave due to the large crowd

I would've had to go through. In my desperation, the boy looked at me and asked, "Do you want to relieve yourself?"

I said, "Yes."

He then placed a cloth over my face (blinding me in effect) and said, "Go and come back quickly. The Salaah is about to begin."

I felt a slight drowsiness and lifted the cloth off my face….to find myself now standing in front of an open doorway! Someone inside said, "Come in."

I walked inside and saw that I was in an elegant palace with every facility available for me. After relieving myself and making wudhu, I heard the voice then ask, "Are you finished?"

I said, "Yes," and thereafter had the cloth placed over my face again. After lifting it up, I was surprised to see that I was now back again in the musjid; same row, same place, same time – as if I hadn't gone anywhere! Even those around me noticed nothing!

I was naturally stunned by this and didn't understand what had just happened. Nevertheless, the congregation stood up to read the Jumaa Salaah and so did I.

After the Salaah, I got up to leave and saw the boy again. He smiled at me and said, "Sahl ﷺ! You probably don't understand what just happened."

I replied, "No, I don't."

He then said, "Come with me."

We then walked together outside until we came to a palace exactly like the one I was in just a few minutes ago. Seeing it *just* the way I left it, I said in amazement, "امنت بالله I believe in Allah ﷻ!"

The boy replied, "Sahl ﷺ! من اطاع الله تعالى اطاعه كل شئ اطلبه تجده Whoever obeys Allah ﷻ is obeyed by everything else. When that person asks for something, he receives it."

I began to cry so much after hearing this that my vision became distorted. When I tried to see again, I saw neither the boy nor the palace in front of me and thereafter decided to dedicate more of my life to the worship of Allah ﷻ." – *Raudul-Riyaaheen, Pg. 105*

Lesson There are certain individuals in the Ummah of our Beloved Prophet ﷺ who have been bestowed with *great* favors by Allah ﷻ, and to deny them is to deny His mercy and benevolence upon them. For example, we learn that it's possible for someone to physically travel great distances in the blink of an eye (beyond the boundaries of space and time). Why should this be surprising when the Prophet ﷺ himself returned after his ascension on the night of Me'raaj to find his bed still warm?

There lived a merchant in Baghdad who used to have great enmity for the Friends of Allah ﷻ. Once, after reading his Jumaa Salaah, he saw the barefoot Hadrat Bishr Haafi ؓ walking out of the musjid as soon as the Salaah was complete and said to himself, "Some Saint he is! He can't wait to leave. Let me follow him and see where he's going."

So, after leaving the musjid, the merchant saw Hadrat Bishr Haafi ؓ going to a baker, purchasing a few pieces of bread and proceeding out of the city of Baghdad. He angrily thought, "He left the musjid so quickly just for some bread…and now he's going to find someplace quiet to sit and eat alone! I'll keep following him until he starts eating, then I'll make myself known and embarrass him."

After following him for some time, they eventually reached a small village, where the merchant saw Hadrat Bishr Haafi ؓ entering its musjid. He peered inside to see what was going on and saw the great Saint sitting by the head of a sick man, feeding him the bread he'd just bought.

Underwhelmed, the merchant then decided to pass some time by taking a short walk around the village. When he later returned to the musjid, however, he found the sick man still there (without Hadrat Bishr ؓ) and asked him, "Where's Bishr Haafi ؓ?"

The man replied, "He went back to Baghdad."

"How far is Baghdad from here?"

"More than a day by foot."

The merchant read "Inna Lillaahi…!" in surprise and thought, "Now I'm stuck here! I didn't notice the distance being *that long* when we arrived. How long until he returns?"

The man answered, "Next Jumaa."

So, the helpless merchant had no choice but to stay in the village the entire week.

As promised, on the following Jumaa, Hadrat Bishr Haafi ؓ arrived to see to the old man again and was told by him, "Hadrat, this poor man followed you from Baghdad last week and has been stuck here for eight days."

The Saint became annoyed upon hearing this and angrily asked the merchant, "Why did you follow me?!"

He miserably replied, "It was my mistake."

Hadrat Bishr Haafi ؓ then said, "Get up and follow me back."

Both then made their way back to the city (in what again felt like a few minutes). When they reached it, Hadrat Bishr Haafi ﷺ turned to the merchant again and cautioned him, saying, "Go home and don't ever do something like that again."

The merchant then repented for ever doubting the Friends of Allah ﷺ and believed in them with a sincere heart from then on. – *Raudul-Riyaaheen, Pg. 118*

Lesson Allah ﷺ has granted His Friends authority over even land and distance. This is why some are seen able to traverse great distances within short periods of time.

130 – A Lion Takes an Order

Some people once approached Hadrat Ibrahim ibn Ad'ham ﷺ and said, "Hadrat, there's a lion sitting on a road refusing to move. Everyone's terrified of it and the road's being closed. What should we do?"

The great Saint proceeded to where the lion was and said to it, "Lion! If you've been ordered to attack any one of us, then carry out your work. Otherwise, leave this area and go back to where you came from."

The lion immediately got up, looked at Hadrat Ibrahim ibn Ad'ham ﷺ and returned to the jungle. – *Raudul-Riyaaheen, Pg. 128*

131 – A Lion Kisses a Saint's Foot

There was once a king who became infuriated with a Friend of Allah ﷺ and locked him inside a lion cage to be mauled to death. When spectators gathered around to witness the event, they saw that as soon as the lion looked at the Saint, it ran towards him, placed its head on the ground and began to lick his feet (as if it was kissing it). This amazed the king and he thereafter decided to let him go.

When the Saint came out of the cage, people asked him, "What was going through your mind when the lion was licking your feet?!"

He replied, "At that time, I was thinking about Islamic law – asking myself whether a lion's saliva is considered impure or not and whether my foot was still clean." – *Raudul-Riyaaheen, Pg. 129*

Lesson Those that fear Allah ﷺ are feared by everything in His creation.

We also come to know that kissing the feet of the Saints is even the practice of *lions*.

132 – A SILENT BOY

Hadrat Zun-Noon Misri ﷺ narrates, "I was once walking in the suburbs of Syria when I noticed a young boy reading Salaah beneath an apple tree in an abandoned area. Intrigued, I decided to sit and wait for a while so that I could speak to him when he was done.

"After he turned his head in Salaam, I said, "As-Salaamu Alaikum. Who are you and why are you living in such a barren place?"

The boy said nothing. When I repeated the question, he wrote the following stanza with his finger on the ground,

منع اللسان عن الكلام لانه ، كهف البلاء دجالب الافات

'The tongue shouldn't speak, as it's
a house of evil and a bringer of calamities.'

فاذ نطقت فكن لربك ذاكرا ، لا تنسه و احمده فى الحالات

*'So, **should** you say something, praise Allah ﷻ,*
never forget Him and remember Him at all times.'

I began to cry upon reading this and wrote the following in reply,

و ما من كاتب الا سبيلى ، و يبقى الدهر ما كتبت يداه

'And what of the writer but that he will soon be tested,
while that which he wrote continues to remain?'

فلا تكتب بكفك غير شئ ، يسوك فى القيامة ان تراه

'So don't write anything by hand,
that which may bring regret to oneself on the Final Day.'

When the boy read this, he let out a wail, fell to the ground and passed away. I began to wonder if I should perform his *ghusl* & *kafn*, but before I could do anything, I heard a voice from the unseen say, "Don't worry about this. His Lord will carry out whatever needs to be done through His angels."

So, I left the boy as he was and walked away.

As I was leaving, I turned around out of curiosity to see if anything was happening and saw that he was no longer there. – *Raudul-Riyaaheen, Pg. 22*

Lesson Absurd, anti-Islamic things should not be said and entertained, and one should be conscious that his every word will soon be reviewed on the Day of Judgment.

133 – SAFETY!

There lived a Saint who used to constantly say, "O Allah ﷻ, safety!"

People once asked him why he did this. He replied, "I was once carrying a bag of wheat and became exhausted because of it. At that very moment, I made the following dua to Allah ﷻ, "O Allah ﷻ, grant me two pieces of bread every day even if I choose not to work for it."

Soon after this, I saw two people fighting and went closer to separate them. One of them swung for the other and hit me instead. When the police arrived, they grabbed all three of us (thinking that I was also involved) and threw us in jail, wherein we were fed two pieces of bread a day.

While inside, I heard a voice say to me, "You are now getting what you asked for. If you wish for safety instead, you will receive it."

I then replied, "O Allah ﷻ, safety!"

So, the following day, I was found innocent and was told to leave." – *Nuzhatul-Majaalis, Vol. 1, Pg. 79*

134 – THE PRICE OF BEAUTY

Hadrat Malik ibn Deenar ؓ was once walking in the markets of Basra when he saw a slave-woman for sale and inquired about her price from her owner. The owner replied, "You're a pious person, so I won't charge you anything."

Hadrat Malik ibn Deenar ؓ then said, "Tell me how much she is anyway. I've paid for slaves pricier than her. She doesn't even look like she's worth anything, and if there *is* a price, it couldn't be anything more than two date-pits. I'm only saying this because she has many faults in her. If she doesn't use perfume for more than two days, a bad smell will start to come out from her body and clothes. Her mouth will give off a stench if she doesn't use *miswaak*, and her hair will have lice if she abandons her comb.

She'll be old after a few years and will never experience a month without menstruation and uncleanliness. Brother! I have completed the sale for someone who's wholly made of *noor*, musk and camphor. The spit from her mouth can turn even the saltiest of rivers sweet, and her smile can bring the dead back to life. Her face is more radiant than the sun, and her garment scents the area around her. She's even been described as,

حور مقصورات في الخيام

"Fair ones, close guarded in pavilions."
– Surah Ar-Rahman (55), Verse 72

in the Quran."

The man asked in surprise, "What would be the price of such a woman?!"

Hadrat Malik ibn Deenar ﷺ replied, "The deserting of one's carnal desires and two rakaats optional Salaah every night."

The man then freed all of the slaves he was selling, gave away everything he had in the path of Allah ﷻ and lived the rest of his life as a devout worshipper. – *Nuzhatul-Majaalis, Vol. 1, Pg. 434*

Lesson The riches of the world are finite and imperfect while the riches of the Hereafter are faultless and for eternity.

We also come to know that giving up one's carnal desires is a source of great reward.

135 – HOW TO SIN FREELY

Someone once approached Hadrat Ibrahim ibn Ad'ham ﷺ and said, "Tell me how I can sin without being accountable for it."

He replied, "If you can do any one of these five things, you are free to do as you wish,

1. Eat that which is not provided by Allah ﷻ,

2. Find a place that is not within His kingdom,

3. Go where He cannot see you,

4. Tell the Angel of Death ﷺ when he comes to you, "Give me some time to repent first,"

5. Or be able to refute the decree given to you on the Day of Judgment (regarding whether you will be an inmate of Jannah or Jahannam)."

Hearing this, the man replied that all of these things are impossible. Hadrat Ibrahim ibn Ad'ham ﷺ then said, "Then ask yourself, which sin are you exempt from?"

The man then fell to the feet of the great Saint and made tauba for having asked such a question. – *Tazkiratul-Auliya, Pg. 120*

Lesson How can we at least not *try* to please Allah ﷺ when we live in His domain and are sustained by that which He provides for us?

136 – A FRIEND IN JANNAH

Hadrat Ibrahim Ad'ham ﷺ once asked in a dua, "O Allah ﷺ, show me who will be my friend in Paradise."

That night, he was told in a dream, "Your partner in Jannah will be a woman named Salaamah who currently grazes cows in a certain pasture near you."

So, Hadrat Ibrahim ﷺ woke up the following morning and headed to the place he was shown. As expected, he found the woman he'd come looking for and greeted her. She answered, "Wa Alaikum-Salaam, Ibrahim ﷺ."

The Saint then asked, "Who told you my name?"

"The One Who told you I'll be your friend in Jannah."

"Give me some advice."

"Always stay awake at night and busy yourself in optional and Tahajjud Salaah, because those who stand in prayer at night are presented in front of their Lord. If you claim to love Allah ﷺ, forsake your sleep." – *Nuzhatul-Majaalis, Vol. 1, Pg. 227*

Lesson Allah ﷺ shares His secrets with many of His chosen servants.

We also see that to abandon one's sleep and occupy oneself in Allah's ﷺ worship has been proven to be exceedingly beneficial for the believers.

137 – THE BEAUTY OF ALLAH ﷺ

A woman once approached Hadrat Junaid Baghdadi ﷺ and said, "Hadrat, my husband wants to marry another woman!"

He replied, "If there aren't four women currently in his nikah, he's allowed to do so."

She then said, "If I was allowed to show you my beauty, I would have, so that you'd see it and say, 'Why would he need to marry someone else when he already has such a beautiful woman in his nikah?'"

Hadrat Junaid Baghdadi ﷺ was immediately taken aback by this statement and began to cry. When the woman asked him why he did so, he explained, "I thought to myself, 'What if Allah ﷻ said to us, "If it was permissible in the world for Me to be seen, I would lift the veil over my splendor so that those who see Me would come to know that when they have such a splendid Lord, what need is there to entertain the love of anyone else in their hearts besides Me?!'" – *Nuzhatul-Majaalis, Vol. 1, Pg. 11*

Lesson How foolish is the one who forsakes Allah ﷻ after having loved and believed in Him?!

138 – THE BLACKBOARD OF A SAINT

A man once visited Hadrat Mansoor Bata'ihi ﷺ and was told, "I see misfortune written on your forehead."

Concerned about this, he then decided to go to Shaikh Ahmed Rumi ﷺ, who saw him, gestured something in the air (as if he was erasing something with his hand) and said, "Read this verse,

يمحو الله ما يشاء و يثبت

"Allah ﷻ removes what He wills and confirms what He wills."
– Surah Ra'd (13), Verse 39

After doing so, the man then went again to Hadrat Mansoor Bata'ihi ﷺ and was told, "By the blessings of Shaikh Ahmed ﷺ, you've been transferred from the pit of misery to the station of fortune." – *Nuzhatul-Majaalis, Vol. 1, Pg. 277*

Lesson Allah ﷻ has granted great authority to His Friends ﷺ, to such an extent that they are even able to change the fate of a person if they so wish.

Hadrat Abdullah ibn Mubaarak ؓ was once battling a non-Muslim in Jihad. As they clashed, the time for Salaah arrived and Hadrat Abdullah ؓ requested a short reprieve from him to fulfill it. The man agreed, and so the great Saint left, read his Salaah, and then returned afterwards.

When the time for the disbeliever's prayer arrived, he too sought permission to fulfill it from Hadrat Abdullah ؓ and was granted permission to do so.

While he was praying facing an idol, Hadrat Abdullah ؓ thought to himself, "I can just kill him now and end this…"

He then drew his sword…and was about to strike the man when he heard a voice say to him, "Abdullah,

اوفوا بالعهد کان مسئولا
"Fulfill (every) engagement, for (every) engagement will be enquired into (on the Last Day)!"
– Surah Isra (17), Verse 34

Hearing this (and with his sword still in the air), Hadrat Abdullah ؓ began to cry.

That moment, the disbeliever completed his prayer, saw this strange scene in front of him and asked what had happened. When Hadrat Abdullah ؓ related the entire incident to him, he too cried in shock and said, "How disgraceful of me to be disobedient to the One Who safeguards even His enemies by reprimanding His friends?!"

He then read the Kalima and became a Muslim! – *Tazkiratul-Auliya, Pg. 171*

Lesson No words can express how much emphasis Islam has placed on the fulfillment of promises.

140 – THE MOUTH OF AN ALCOHOLIC

Hadrat Ibrahim ibn Ad'ham ؓ was once walking along a pathway when he saw a drunk man collapse on the side of the road, jabbering away in his demented state. The great Saint stopped alongside him and said, "This tongue was supposed to be used for the remembrance of Allah ﷻ. What could possibly have happened to it that it's now used to speak nonsense?!"

He then called for water, washed the mouth of the man and walked away.

When the man returned to his senses, he was told what had happened by those around him, and so he began to cry and said, "O Allah ﷻ! I make tauba to You with a sincere heart. Through Your close friend (Hadrat Ibrahim ibn Ad'ham ﷺ), I ask You to forgive me."

That night, Hadrat Ibrahim ﷺ was told in a dream, "O Ibrahim, you washed the mouth of an alcoholic in Our consideration, so We washed his heart for you." – *Raudul-Riyaaheen, Pg. 117*

Lesson Closeness to the Friends of Allah ﷻ may assist one in being forgiven and even have one's fate changed if Allah ﷻ so wills. How unfortunate, then, are those who ask why we should travel great distances to present ourselves in front of the Saints?!

141 – TRUTHFULNESS

The tyrant king of his time, Hajaaj ibn Yusuf, once saw a man making tawaaf around the Kaaba and became drawn to him. So, he returned to his court, summoned his guards and ordered them to bring the man to him.

When the man (who was a Friend of Allah ﷻ) came inside, he stood in front of the king (with a lack of interest) and was asked,

"Who are you?"

He replied, "A Muslim from amongst Muslims."

"That's not what I meant. I meant where do you come from?"

"I come from Yemen."

"The governor of Yemen is my brother, Muhammad ibn Yusuf. How do you see him?"

"He's a man of commanding stature and wears fine clothes."

"I meant how do you see him in his actions?"

"He's a sinner, obedient only to the desires of his people and not to the desires of his Lord."

Hajaaj ibn Yusuf replied, "Such abuse! Didn't I just tell you how I'm associated to him?! I'm his brother!"

The Saint answered, "But don't you know how I'm associated to Allah ﷻ? I'm His servant. I came to visit His house, and I confirm the truth of His Prophet ﷺ!"

The king became silent upon hearing this, and (without seeking his permission) the man then turned around and walked away. – *Raudul-Riyaaheen, Pg. 115*

Lesson The Friends of Allah ﷻ fear nothing but Him and are not afraid to speak honestly and openly in front of even the kings of their time. This is why corrupt rulers were always afraid of them.

142 – JAIL TO GARDEN

A young Saint once advised the carrying out of a good deed and the stopping of a bad one. When the Khalifa of his time, Haroon Rashid, came to know of this, he ordered for the boy to be caught and thrown into a windowless jail cell wherein he would wither away and die.

For this reason, the boy was seized and placed in such a room.

The following morning, people saw him walking in a public garden and immediately informed the Khalifa of this. When the boy was seized once again, Haroon Rashid summoned him to his court and asked him, "Who let you out of the jail?!"

He replied, "The One Who took me to the garden."

"Then who took you to the garden?"

"The One Who let me out of the jail."

The ruler then lost all hope in questioning him and said, "This is a strange matter."

The boy replied, "For Allah ﷻ, such a thing is neither strange nor difficult."

Hearing this, Haroon Rashid began to cry and thereafter showed great respect to the boy by honoring him with one of his special robes and seating him upon a horse. He then told one of his men to walk him around the city shouting out the following message, "This is a servant of Allah ﷻ

who has been shown tremendous favour by Him! Our ruler wished to disgrace him but was unable to do so!" – *Raudul-Riyaaheen, Pg. 104*

Lesson The Friends of Allah ﷻ are protected by Him and so cannot be disgraced by anyone in creation. On the contrary, those who wish to do so will only and eventually disgrace themselves. To wage war with them is in fact waging war with Allah ﷻ. May Allah ﷻ instill within us the love and respect of His close and chosen servants. Aameen.

143 – A PALACE FIT FOR A KING

A king once had a very extravagant palace built for him. To celebrate its completion, he sent out an open invitation to the public and invited many of his friends and followers for a feast within.

While they all ate, he said to the gathering, "Let me know of any fault you see in the design of this building."

All replied that it was complete and without any imperfection.

One man, however (who was a Friend of Allah ﷻ), said nothing. When the king asked him the same question, he replied, "It has two faults."

The king asked, "And what are they?"

The Saint replied, "One, that the building will one day perish. And two, that its inhabitant will one day die."

The king then asked, "So is there any palace without these two faults?"

He replied, "Yes, in Jannah."

The Saint then delivered such a moving lecture, instilling the love of Jannah and the fear of Jahannam into the gathering, that the king began to cry, retired from his kingship and committed the rest of his life to the remembrance of Allah ﷻ." – *Raudul-Riyaaheen, Pg. 108*

Lesson This world is finite while the treasures of the Hereafter are far greater and for eternity. Man should not attach himself to this life.

144 – EXAMINATION

There once lived a king who wanted to test the insight of the Friends of Allah ﷻ, so he invited some of them to his court for a feast and said to some of his friends, "Let's see if these 'Saints' can distinguish between Halaal and Haraam."

So, when the guests were seated, the king and his friends sat with them and all waited to be served. At that moment, one of the Saints said, "Today, I'll be the servant."

He then stood up, fetched the food and returned to the table, placing the plates of Haraam food in front of the king & his friends and the plates of Halaal food in front of the pious individuals, saying afterwards,

الطيبات للطيبين و الخبيثات للخبيثين
"Purity for the pure and uncleanliness for the unclean."

Hearing this, the king sincerely repented for his ways, confessed to his scheme and became a true believer in the Friends of Allah ﷻ. – *Raudul-Riyaaheen, Pg. 228*

Lesson The knowledge of the Saints is vast, and nothing is hidden from their sight (including the state of things, e.g. what is Halaal and Haraam). This is all due to their following of the Beloved Prophet of Allah ﷺ. So, if the Holy Prophet's ﷺ followers were so informed of what was happening in the world, what can now be said of the knowledge of the Holy Prophet ﷺ himself?!

145 – DELIVERY

A leading merchant of Baghdad was once sitting in a musjid with a very pious and handsome individual who lifted up his hands in dua and said, "O Allah ﷻ, give me roasted meat and sweetmeats."

The merchant thought, "He's really just trying to tell me to get it for him. By Allah ﷻ, if he'd asked me directly, I would have, but now I won't."

The pious man then lay down and fell asleep. A short while later, someone entered the musjid with a covered tray, laid it next to the man and woke him up, saying, "Here's the food you asked for. Eat."

So, the Saint got up, partook in some of it and gave the tray back.

Seeing this, the merchant stopped the bringer of the food as he was leaving and asked him in confusion, "What's this all about?!"

He replied, "I recently received a lot of money, so my wife requested that we prepare some meat and sweetmeats for ourselves. Before we could eat it, I decided to take a quick nap and was told by the Holy Prophet ﷺ in a dream, 'There's a Friend of Allah ﷻ in the musjid who asked for this food. Give him some of it first and you'll receive Jannah in return.' So, I came here immediately...and I'm happy to have received Jannah by doing so."

The merchant asked him, "How much did this food cost?"

He replied, "Two dinaars."

"Here's two. Take it and let me have some of that reward."

The man replied, "No."

"Okay. Then take 10 dinaars."

"No!"

"One hundred then!"

The man finally said, "Even for the *treasures of the Earth*, I wouldn't share what I've received from the Prophet 🌸 with you. Had it been in your fate, you would have preceded me in attaining it, but for now, you are unworthy. – *Raudul-Riyaaheen, Pg. 153*

Lesson The Friends of Allah 🌸 are granted whatever they wish, and Allah 🌸 channels it to his beloved servants through the intervention of the Holy Prophet 🌸.

146 – A WOMAN FULL OF NOOR

Hadrat Zun-Noon 🌸 states, "I was once making tawaaf around the Kaaba when I saw a beam of Noor shining up to the sky. After fulfilling my obligation, I followed it to its source and saw that it was coming from a radiant woman holding onto the covering of the Kaaba saying,

انت تدری من حبیبی ، من حبیبی انت تدری
'You (O Kaaba) know Who I love.

قد کتمت الحب حتی ، ضاق بالکتمان صدری
My heart has tightened for hiding it.'

She then began to cry and made the following dua, "O Allah 🌸, I present the love *You have for me*. Grant me forgiveness."
I interrupted her by saying, "O servant of Allah 🌸, how do *you* know Allah 🌸 loves You? Say 'I present the love *I have for You*' instead."

She replied, "Zun-Noon 🌼. Haven't you read the verse of the Quran,

فسوف ياتى الله بقوم يحبهم و يحبونه

"Soon Allah 🌼 will produce a people whom He will love as they will love Him."
– Surah Ma'ida (5), Verse 54

"See? Allah 🌼 mentioned His love first, saying that He will love them and *then* they will love Him. So, those who will eventually love Allah 🌼 in their lifetimes will be loved by Him first."

I then asked her, "How do you know my name?"

She replied, "Why should the one who knows the Creator not know the creation?"

After that, she asked me to look in a certain direction, and when I did, I saw nothing, turned around again and found that she had disappeared. – *Raudul-Riyaaheen, Pg. 219*

Lesson The Friends of Allah 🌼 are deeply loved by Him and are granted a special Noor no ordinary individual possesses.

We also come to know that they are granted great knowledge of the universe. What can now be said of their teachers, the Prophets themselves?!

147 – A YOUNG BOY

Hadrat Abdullah ibn Dāsān 🌼 narrates, "I once saw a young boy crying in the markets of Basra and asked him, "Why are you crying?"

He replied, "In fear of the fire of Jahannam."

I then asked, "You're so young, what are you afraid of?"

He answered, "I saw my mother burning big pieces of wood in her stove by placing smaller sticks beneath them. Maybe Allah 🌼 will use minors like me to burn the Fire for the sinners."

I was very affected by these words and thereafter asked him if he'd like to stay with me. He replied, "I will on four conditions: that I'm fed when I'm hungry, that my thirst is quenched when I'm thirsty, that I'm forgiven when I sin, and that I'm raised back to life after my demise."

I replied, "I cannot do all of these things."

The boy then said, "Then carry on with your work. I'll stay with the One Who can." – *Raudul-Riyaaheen, Pg. 94*

Lesson In previous times, the fear of Allah ﷻ was instilled into even children. Today, it's difficult to find even *adults* who have this quality in them.

148 – CHANGING RESIDENCE

Hadrat Ahmed ibn Mansoor ☀ narrates, "My teacher, Hadrat Abul-Ya'qub Musa ☀, once told me that one of his disciples had passed away, and that while he gave him ghusl, the body grabbed his thumb as it lay there (while the ghusl continued as normal). After some time, he said to him, "Son, leave my thumb. I know you're not dead, but have merely moved from one place to another."

Hearing this, the body then let go. – *Raudul-Riyaaheen, Pg. 71*

Lesson After completing the order of Allah ﷻ (that every *nafs* will taste death), the Friends of Allah ﷻ are immediately returned to life to live in peace in the Hereafter.

149 – THE WELL

Hadrat Abdullah ibn Haneef ☀ narrates, "I once left my home to perform Hajj and chose not to stop in Baghdad along the way (thinking that I would go to meet Hadrat Junaid Baghdadi ☀ on my return). As I continued, I began to feel extremely thirsty and eventually found a well which a deer was drinking out of. Nevertheless, I was relieved to have finally found some water and waited for the deer to finish.

When it left, I approached the well but was surprised to see that the water had now receded! I then turned around in sadness and walked away thinking, "I haven't even reached the rank of a deer."

Immediately, a voice said to me, "Impatient person! You were being tested but you chose impatience instead. Go back and drink as you please."

So, when I returned to the well, I saw that the water was now right at the top, so I drank to my heart's content and also filled my water-bag (which didn't finish even until Madina).

After the Hajj, I passed Baghdad again and went to see the great Shaikh, Hadrat Junaid Baghdadi ☀. As soon as he saw me, he said, "Abdullah ☀, if only you'd waited at the well, the water would've flown to your feet." – *Raudul-Riyaaheen, Pg. 71*

Lesson Sitting in Baghdad, the Friends of Allah ﷻ know what is happening miles away, while sitting in our homes, we don't even know what is happening *inside*!

150 – EVEN ANIMALS AS SLAVES

Hadrat Abu Ayub Hammāl ؓ states that whenever Hadrat Abu Abdullah Dailmi ؓ would travel, he wouldn't tie his donkey to any post, but would rather say to it, "Go. Eat or drink whatever you want and then return at this specific time."

As instructed, the donkey would leave, go into the jungle and return the time it was ordered. – *Raudul-Faa'iq, Pg. 72*

151 – MONEY FOR THE JOURNEY

Hadrat ibn Abi Ayaas ؓ states, "We were in Askalaan when a young boy approached us and sat down to deliver a tremendous talk. One day, he said that he was leaving for Alexandria, and so, because I was so fascinated with him, I decided to go with.

During our trip, I offered him the money I'd come with but he declined. When I insisted he take it, he simply ignored me, placed some sand & water into a bowl and mixed it. He then gave it to me and said, "Drink."

I did as I was told…and found that it was the sweetest water I'd ever tasted!

The boy then turned to me and said, "When things are like this, who needs money?" – *Raudul-Faa'iq, Pg. 72*

152 – SHEEP AND WOLVES RECONCILE

Hadrat Abdullah ibn Zaid ؓ narrates, "I once made the following dua three nights in a row, "O Allah ﷻ, tell me who will be my friend in Jannah."

On the third night, I heard a voice say to me, "Your friend will be a woman named Maimoona, a resident of Kufa."

So, I traveled to Kufa to meet this woman and asked the people about her. They replied, "She's an odd woman who grazes our sheep until the evening."

After being given directions, I made my way towards the pasture and found the woman busy in Salaah. As I waited, I was surprised to see sheep and wolves walking amongst each other nearby – neither were the sheep afraid of the wolves nor were the wolves interested in attacking the sheep!

Maimoona 🕮 then completed her Salaah and said to me, "Abdullah 🕮! It will be in *Jannah* where we will be friends, not here."

I asked her, "Who told you my name?"

She answered, "The One Who told you about me."

I then asked, "Tell me, since when did these wolves submit to these sheep?"

She replied, "The day Maimoona 🕮 submitted to her Lord." – *Raudul-Faa'iq, Pg. 73*

153 – THE FAVOURS OF ALLAH 🕮

A Friend of Allah 🕮 once saw an arrogant person riding a horse and asked him why he displayed so much vanity. He replied, "I'm a trusted friend and confidant of the king. I even feed him when he's hungry, and for all this, he looks at me with great fondness at least 3 times a day."

The Saint asked, "And what if you make a mistake?"

He replied, "I'd be whipped to death."

The Saint then said, "If that's the case, I should be prouder than you, because I serve a King who feeds me, quenches my thirst, guards me while I sleep and even consoles me when I'm alone. If I do something wrong, He forgives me; and every day, He looks at me at least 360 times with affection and mercy."

This had a great effect on the man. He therefore descended from his horse and said, "Make me the servant of this King too." – *Nuzhatul-Majaalis, Vol. 1, Pg. 440*

Lesson The favours and mercy shown by Allah 🕮 to his servants cannot be equaled even by those shown by a king in a lifetime.

154 – YOU SPEAK THE TRUTH

Hadrat Sayed Muhammad Yemeni 🕮 had a son who was born a Friend of Allah 🕮. Once, when he was three years old, he walked out of the house, sat in his father's workplace and ordered someone to write, "فلان فى الجنة" (So-and-so) is in Jannah."

The order was carried out and thereafter repeated; and in this way, many names of people destined for Jannah were written down.

The boy then said, "Write: فلان فى النار (So-and-so) is in the fire."

This time, however, the writer declined, and after being ordered by the boy another three times to do so, he still refused and was eventually told, "انت فى النار *You* are in the fire!"

In fright, the man then ran to Hadrat Sayed Muhammad Yemeni ؓ and told him what his son had just said. The Saint replied, "I cannot change his statement, but you do have a choice. You can either choose the fire of the world or the fire of the Hereafter."

The man replied, "I prefer the fire of the world."

In an instant, he then burst into flames and died where he was. – *Malfoozaat of Imam Ahmed Raza* ؓ, *Vol. 1, Pg. 18*

Lesson According to, "لو اقسم على الله لا بره If He takes an oath on Allah ﷻ, He fulfils it," Allah ﷻ carries out the statements of his beloved Friends ؓ to protect their integrity and safeguard them from being classified as liars. For this reason, we should constantly seek the pleasure of the Saints and request them to make dua for us.

155 – PITCHER OF WATER

Hadrat Sirri Saqti ؓ was once fasting and left some water in a jug so that it would be cool by Maghrib. During the time of Asr, he sat in deep contemplation of Allah ﷻ and began to see maidens of Jannah passing by one-by-one in front of him. He asked them, "Who are you for?" and each replied that they were for a certain person.

At that moment one of them came forward, and the Saint asked her the same question. She replied, "I'm for the one who doesn't store cool water while fasting."

Hadrat Sirri Saqti ؓ then said, "If you're true in what you say, drop the jar."

He then opened his eyes due to a loud sound he'd heard and saw that it came from the jar that was now overturned. – *Malfoozaat, Pg. 86*

Lesson The Saints try as hard as possible to trade what is good in the world for what is good in the Hereafter, even if what they are doing is not classified as a sin.

A beggar once requested a shopkeeper to give him some money. When the shopkeeper said that he wouldn't, the man replied, "Give me some money or I'll turn this shop upside-down!"

A crowd began to gather around this scene. In the commotion, a pious and accepted man of the public came forward and said to the shopkeer, "Give him the money quick or your shop will be destroyed!"

The people asked him, "Hadrat, what can this ignorant beggar possibly do?!"

He replied, "I looked inside him and saw nothing, so I initially thought the same thing. Then I decided to look in his Shaikh and also found nothing, but when I looked inside his grand-Shaikh, I found him to be from amongst the pious servants of Allah ﷻ, standing in wait for the order to turn the shop upside-down." – *Malfoozaat, Vol. 1, Pg. 14*

Lesson Being connected to a Friend of Allah ﷻ in any way will undoubtedly prove beneficial even to the most ordinary of men. So, one should sincerely seek a Murshid in one's life and submit to him in hope that one may be perfected someday through his assistance.

157 – THIS OLD SERVANT OF YOURS

There was a Friend of Allah ﷻ who became very old and weak and once fell while reading Esha Salaah, bruising himself in the process. After the Salaah, he lifted up his hands in dua and said, "O Allah ﷻ! I'm weak now. Kings free their servants from duty when they are old, so I ask You to free me too."

This dua was accepted, and so, when the Saint woke up the following morning, he was found to be mentally unsound (since Islamic duties are only compulsory on the sane). – *Malfoozaat, Vol. 1, Pg. 82*

Lesson Neither in their youth nor in their old age do the Friends of Allah ﷺ abandon their duties to Allah ﷻ.

We also come to know that once a person is sane and mature, he is obligated to read Salaah. How foolish and unfortunate then is the person who doesn't read it even when he's of sound health?!

Hadrat Sayed Ahmed Jaam Zinda Pīr ﷺ was once traveling and came across a group of people gathered around a dead elephant on the side of the road. He asked them, "What's this?"

They replied, "A dead elephant."

He then asked, "How could it have died while its trunk, its eyes and its feet are like this?"

As soon as he said this, the elephant came to life, got up and walked away. This is why the great Saint was known as 'Zinda Pīr'. – *Malfūzaat, Vol. 1, Pg. 16*

Lesson Just as how Allah ﷻ granted Hadrat Esa ﷺ the power to give life to the dead, so too are some of the Saints blessed with such a quality. How then can someone claim to be equal to, not just a person who has life *in* him, but one who *gives life* to others?

159 – THREE QALANDARS

Three Qalandars came to the court of Hadrat Nizaamul-Haqq Mehboob Ilaahi ﷺ and requested food from him. So, he ordered his servant to see to them.

When the food was brought and placed before them, one of the men threw it aside and said, "Bring better food."

Hadrat Nizaamul-Haqq ﷺ thought nothing of this act of indecency and remained silent.

A short while later, food better than the first was brought, and again, the man picked up his plate and threw it away, saying, "Bring better food!"

After the third serving was brought and also thrown aside, Hadrat Nizaamul-Haqq ﷺ called the man towards him and said in his ear, "This food is better than the dead ox you just ate."

The man was shocked upon hearing this! Along the way, he and his two friends found a dead ox on the side of the road (complete with maggots) and decided to eat it (since they were starving).

The man then fell at the feet of Hadrat Mehboob Ilaahi ﷺ but was lovingly picked up by him and embraced. After that, the Saint granted him whatever he wished to bestow. – *Malfoozaat, Vol. 1, Pg. 12*

Lesson The Friends of Allah ﷻ are aware of the occurrences in creation and reveal this in times of necessity.

160 – FEELINGS OF THE HEART

A king once visited a Friend of Allah ﷻ and was offered a bowl of apples by him. He replied, "Hadrat, eat with me," and so, both began to partake in it.

As they ate, the king saw a single apple which stood out amongst the rest and thought to himself, "If he picks up that apple and gives it to me, I'll know he's a Friend of Allah ﷻ."

The Saint then picked up the apple, held it in his hands and said, "I was in Egypt some time ago and attended a very big fair there. There was a man who had a donkey with a cloth tied over its eyes. He'd take something that belonged to someone, give it to someone else and then tell the donkey to go look for it. The donkey would then search the entire fair, find the person who had the item, and prop its head up in front of him. The item was then returned to its rightful owner. I'm telling you this story because, if I eat the apple, I'm not a Saint to you, but if I give it to you, what have I done greater than the donkey?"

The Saint then gave the apple to the king. – *Malfoozaat, Vol. 1, Pg. 10*

Lesson The Friends of Allah ﷺ are aware of the thoughts of people but still don't consider themselves eminent for it.

161 – A STANZA'S REPLY

The father of Amir Khusroo ﷺ once took him and his brother to become disciples of Hadrat Khwaja Nizamuddin Auliya ﷺ. As they entered the great Saint's workplace, Amir Khusroo ﷺ said to his father, "I won't just blindly become the disciple (مرید) of someone I don't know. You two go inside and I'll wait here."

So, his father and brother proceeded inside while the young boy sat at the door, writing the following stanza in the Persian language, "O Khwaja Nizamuddin ﷺ! Your residence is so magnificent that even if a pigeon rests on its roof, it becomes a bird of prey. Today a traveler has come to your doorstep. What is your order? Should he enter or not?"

He then thought to himself, "If he's truly a Friend of Allah ﷻ, he will give me a reply."

At that very moment (while inside) Hadrat Khwaja Nizamuddin ؓ told his servant to leave the room and say the following to the boy outside (also a stanza in the Persian language), "If Amir ؓ is a man of truth, he should come in and be with us for a short while. If he's a fool, he should go back to where he came from."

Hearing this, Amir Khusroo ؓ immediately got up and presented himself in front of the great Saint. – *Mughniul-Waaizeen, Pg. 224*

Lesson The Friends of Allah ﷻ being aware of the thoughts of an individual is only *one* reason why they shouldn't be disrespected (even at heart).

162 – DISTRUST

A superior of Lahore once sent 100 dinars to Hadrat Baba-Fareeduddin Ganj Shakar ؓ through his friend, Shahaabuddin Ghaznawi.

While taking it to him, Shahaabuddin decided to keep half of it and presented Hadrat Baba-Fareeduddin ؓ with only 50 dinars. The Saint accepted the money but then said, "Shahaabuddin, you have distributed it equally in brotherhood. This sort of thing is not becoming of a man of piety."

Hearing this, Shahaabuddin immediately presented the other half to the great Saint. Hadrat Baba-Fareeduddin ؓ nevertheless allowed him to keep *all* of the 100 dinars but said, "The only reason this occurred is because breach of trust is a major sin and invalidates the worship of the one who commits it."

Shahaabuddin then became the disciple of Hadrat a second time. – *Mughniul-Waaizeen, Pg. 224*

163 – SURRENDER

When Khwaja Moeenuddin Chishti ؓ reached India, he stayed in Delhi for a few days and was informed by one of his disciples that he was being unjustly mistreated by the Indian king (who was at that time Rai Pithūra). In response, the Saint sent a letter to Rai Pithūra ordering him not to do such a thing.

When the letter reached the king, he read it and then said to his court, "This foreigner informs others of the unseen but he's still nothing in front of me."

Khwaja Moeenuddin ◉ was later informed of this arrogant reply and said out loud, "We took hold of Rai Pithūra in his reign and now surrender him to the Islamic army."

This statement proved to be true, for, some time later, the army of Sultaan Shahaabuddin Ghauri advanced to the country from Ghazni and eventually overtook the Indian government. – *Iqtibaasul-Anwaar, Pg. 128*

Lesson Whatever is said by the Friends of Allah ◉ becomes true.

We also come to know that denying their knowledge (even that of the unseen) earns one their anger and (subsequently) the anger of Allah ◉. When Allah ◉ has taken them as His Friends, how can ordinary Muslims harbor enmity towards them?!

164 – A Pious Descendant of the Prophet ◉

A group of learned scholars, each distinguished in their academic field, once approached a descendant of the Holy Prophet ◉ and said, "We came to test your knowledge."

Knowing that the man had no academic background, the scholars wished to belittle him and show that piety doesn't truly benefit anyone intellectually. So, one by one, they asked him questions from a wide range of topics but the man answered them all (sometimes looking to the left and sometimes to the right before giving his reply).

The scholars soon realized that they were beaten and walked away in shame. Someone then approached the man and asked, "Why were you looking either left or right before answering?"

He replied, "When I saw those people approaching me, I made the following dua, 'O Allah ◉! Let me not be disgraced by them.' So, in reply, Allah ◉ placed the soul of Imam Abu Hanifa ◉ on my right and the soul of Shaikh Bu Ali Seena on my left. Whenever I was asked any question of the sciences, I referred to Imam Abu Hanifa ◉, and whenever I was asked any question of philosophy, I referred to Shaikh Bu Ali Seena ◉. – *Risaalat al-Ibqaa, April 1950 by Maulvi Ashraf Ali Thanwi*

Lesson This incident (narrated by a well-known Deobandi leader) confirms the belief that the Friends of Allah ◉ are able to assist us even *after* their demise by the command of Allah ◉. If this is now proven to be the authority granted by Allah ﷻ to the Saints, can one now imagine the authority granted by Him to His Beloved Prophet ﷺ?!

165 – THE ABDĀL

Someone once came to Shah Abdul-Aziz ⁣⁣⁣ﷺ and complained, "Today the city of Delhi is relaxed."

He replied, "That's because the *Abdaal* (a certain category of Saints) who currently oversees it is relaxed."

The man asked, "Who's the Abdaal of Delhi?"

Shah Abdul-Aziz ⁣ﷺ replied, "Someone who sells melons in the fruit market."

For this reason, the man proceeded to the market and tried to test the Abdaal by breaking and tasting all of the melons he was selling and placing them back in the basket, saying that he didn't like any of them. Yet, even after leaving them aside and walking away, the Saint said nothing in reply.

A few days later, the man went again to Shah Abdul-Aziz ⁣ﷺ and said, "The city is now operating nicely. Who's the Abdaal now?"

Shah Abdul-Aziz ⁣ﷺ replied, "A man who serves water to people in Chandni Chauk. He takes a small amount as payment."

And so, once again, the man proceeded to the market, found the Abdaal and requested a jug of water from him. When he was given one, he threw it on the floor and said that there was some grass in it (before requesting another).

The Abdaal asked the man, "Can you pay for another one?"

He replied, "No."

The Saint then slapped him and said, "Do you take me for the melon-seller?!" – *Ta'deebul-Ma'siyyah, Pg. 12 by Maulvi Ashraf Ali Thanwi*

Lesson The Friends of Allah ⁣ﷺ are the spiritual governors of the world and are aware of the happenings around them.

166 – AMASSING WEALTH FOR THE SAKE OF ISLAM

In his search for a spiritual guide (مرشد), Maulana Jaami ⁣ﷺ came to the door of Hadrat Khwaja Ubaidullah Ahraar ⁣ﷺ and saw him surrounded with pomp and show, complete with the treasures of the world. In deep regret, he uncontrollably said "*He is not a man, the one who takes the world as his friend*" and then left to lie down in the musjid.

In his dream, he saw himself on the plains of Qiyaamat being hassled by someone requesting payment for an outstanding debt of his. Hadrat Khwaja Ubaidullah Ahraar ؓ (the Saint he'd seen earlier) then approached him with great splendor and asked, "Why did you take what belonged to his man? Pay him from the goods we collected."

Maulana Jaami ؓ then awoke and saw Hadrat Khwaja Ubaidullah Ahraar ؓ coming towards the musjid. He immediately ran to him, placed his head at the feet of the great Saint and said, "Hadrat, forgive me for what I said earlier!"

Hadrat Khwaja Ubaidullah Ahraar ؓ replied, "What was that stanza again?"

"It was a mistake."

"Say it one more time."

"He is not a man, the one who takes the world as his friend."

Hadrat Khwaja Ubaidullah Ahraar ؓ then said, "True, but you should add the following after it, *"If he **does** keep it close, he only keeps it for his friend."* – Da'wate-Abdiyyat by Maulvi Ashraf Ali Thanwi*

Lesson We learn that the money amassed for Islamic work and for the needy is not considered the hoarding of wealth.

167 – THE GREATEST OF HELPERS

Though Hadrat Sayed Ahmed Kabir Rifaa'i ؓ is a famous Saint in the history of Islam, his fame still doesn't equal that of Ghousul-A'zam, Shaikh Abdul-Qadir Jilaani ؓ.

Once, a man came to Shaikh Abdul-Qadir Jilaani ؓ to become a disciple of his and was told, "Brother, I see wretchedness apparent on your forehead. How could you be a disciple of mine?"

The man then went to Hadrat Sayed Ahmed Kabir Rifaa'i ؓ and was told, "Brother, it's the same for me." – *Al-Izaafaatul-Yaumiyya, 1351 A.H, by Maulwi Ashraf Ali Thanwi*

Lesson The original text of this extract acknowledges the famous title bestowed upon Shaikh Abdul-Qadir Jilaani ؓ (i.e. 'Ghousul-Azam'), meaning 'The Greatest of Helpers' (amongst the Friends of Allah ﷻ).

و صلى الله تعالى على سيدنا محمد و اله و صحبه اجمعين

امين برحمتك يا ارحم الراحمين

INDEX
(by Story)

* Mentioned as a reference only (not in the story).

** First name only mentioned (possibly referring to another individual) or ambiguous.

REFERENCES

1. Surah Tauba, Verse 119
2. Maqāsid-e-Hasana
3. Surah A'raaf, Verse 179
4. Surah Nisaa, Verse 59
5. Surah Ma'ida, Verse 35
6. Surah Zāriyāt, Verse 1
7. Surah Zāriyāt, Verse 2
8. Surah Zāriyāt, Verse 3
9. Surah Zāriyāt, Verse 4
10. Surah Nāzi'āt, Verse 74
11. Surah Isra, Verse 12
12. Surah Qāf, Verse 38
13. Surah Mulk, Verse 3
14. Surah Hāqah, Verse 17
15. Surah Naml, Verse 48
16. Surah Baqarah, Verse 196
17. Surah Yusuf, Verse 4
18. Surah Fussilāt, Verse 11
19. Surah Yusuf, Verse 18
20. Surah Baqarah, Verse 113
21. Surah Luqmān, Verse 19
22. Surah Yusuf, Verse 28
23. Surah Nahl, Verse 68
24. Surah Tāhā, Verse 82

OTHER TITLES AVAILABLE

The Beloved's Majesty
Quranic Verses in Praise of the Holy Prophet
(330 Pages)

Our major publication for 2012

Gain a deeper understanding & appreciation of the Holy Quran!

Book includes: Commentary on 100+ verses of the Holy Quran demonstrating the praise of the Holy Prophet 🌸 in over 320 pages.

Covering famous events in the Holy Prophet's 🌸 life, including his creation, advent, childhood, Ascension (Mi'raj), rank on the Day of Judgment, etc. along with many of his qualities, such as his miracles, knowledge, status, authority, praiseworthiness, character, etc.

Referencing major works throughout Islamic History, including Bukhari, Muslim, Tirmidhi, Tafseer Kabeer, Tafseer Roohul-Bayaan, Khazaainul-Irfaan, Madaarijun-Nubuwwah, and many others.

Book also includes two supplementary commentaries dealing with the Friends of Allah 🌸 and the Martyrs of Islam, both substantiated from the Quran.

Learn of the matchless relationship between the Creator and His Beloved Messenger 🌸 from the words of Allah 🌸 Himself!

Stories of the Prophets
(152 Pages)

Over 125 stories covering a range of Prophets throughout Islamic History, with a handy lesson section at the end that explains the beliefs and etiquette that can be derived from them.

Avaible as a free e-book.

The Holy Prophet's 🕌 Kingdom
(72 Pages)

How much did Allah grant His Most Beloved?
A book detailing the great favour shown by Allah to His Beloved Messenger 🕌, sourcing Quranic verses, Ahadith, Verdicts of major Islamic Scholars throughout History, and even rational proofs.
Book also contains a Q&A section covering 11 popular objections on the issue.

The Authority of the Hadith
(24 Pages)

A brief, general reply to those who refute or undermine the Hadith's necessity and integrity. Includes evidence from the Quran of our need for the Hadith, along with rational proofs and a Q&A section dealing with common arguments against the belief.

Available as a free e-book.

www.ingramcontent.com/pod-product-compliance
Lightning Source LLC
LaVergne TN
LVHW011205080426
835508LV00007B/613